D0235835

STORIES FOR KIDS WHO DARE TO BE DIFFERENT

First published in Great Britain in 2018 by

Quercus Editions Ltd
Carmelite House
50 Victoria Embankment
London
EC4Y 0DZ

An Hachette UK company

A CIP catalogue record for this book is available from the British Library

HB ISBN 978 1 78747 652 3

10 9 8 7 6 5 4 3 2 1

Illustrations by Quinton Winter
Inside design by sarahgreeno.com
Printed and bound in Italy by Lego

Stories for Kids who Dare to be Different

TRUE TALES OF BOYS AND GIRLS WHO STOOD UP AND STOOD OUT

BEN BROOKS

ILLUSTRATED BY QUINTON WINTER

Quercus

ADELINE TIFFANIE SUWANA

(BORN 1996)

Every year, the floods crept closer and closer to Adeline's house in Indonesia. Most kids would get excited – flooding meant school was cancelled and they could spend the day playing – but one day the water burst through Adeline's garden fence and rushed into her house.

Her family had to hurriedly move everything important upstairs. When the electricity and running water were cut off, they had to leave their home altogether.

Adeline wanted to know why this was happening.

Her research taught her two things: one, global warming was causing water levels around the world to rise, increasing flooding. And two, the mangrove swamps of North Jakarta were being destroyed, which meant the giant networks of thick roots that had previously been there to absorb the impact of waves and wind were gone.

The mangrove swamps also provided habitats for many animals, filtered out pollution, and attracted different kinds of wildlife that could be harvested or eaten by local people. Their disappearance was felt by everyone.

One school holiday, Adeline gathered 150 friends and classmates to plant mangrove saplings throughout a wildlife sanctuary. While planting, the kids encountered monkeys, snakes and lizards. They found themselves having fun, learning, and connecting with nature.

That day marked the birth of an organization that Adeline called Friends of Nature. Since then, it's gone on to engage more than 25,000 students in over one hundred activities meant to preserve the natural world. They've planted coral in reefs to attract fish and promote eco-tourism, convinced hundreds of people to switch from driving cars to riding bikes, and set up remote villages with electricity generators that run on water.

Adeline believes that young people can be the environmental heroes of their own communities. By stepping up before it's too late, we can help keep ourselves, and our planet, strong and healthy.

ADAM RIPPON

(BORN 1989)

Adam didn't want to go on the ice at first. It took a lot of encouragement from his mother before he'd even put on a pair of skates. Once he did, he found he loved it, and soon she was driving him for hours every week to get to lessons. He was ten years old.

When he first moved away from home to concentrate on skating full-time, Adam had no money at all. He lived off free apples from his gym and slept in his trainer's basement. Then things started going well, and Adam was winning medals and championships. He was gliding, leaping, and pirouetting across the ice like no one else, and it seemed as though he was unstoppable.

Until he hit a roadblock. Adam finished eighth at nationals, which was amazing but it meant he wouldn't make it to the Olympics. Then he landed badly during a practice session and broke his foot. Adam thought about quitting altogether. But while taking a break to work on routines for other skaters, he remembered how much he loved the sport, and realized there was no way he could give it up.

A few years later, he had won one of three spots on the US men's Olympic team. He became the oldest first-time Olympic figure skater and the first openly gay American athlete to compete. Being gay isn't important to the skating, but what is important to Adam is to make it a little more normal, so that kids everywhere have the courage to be who they are.

'I'm like a witch, and you can't kill me!' Adam said. 'I keep coming back every year, and every year I get better.'

Adam has a skating move named after him: the Rippon Lutz. How do you do it? Three backwards jumps in a row with your arms held over your head.

ANA NZINGA MBANDE

(1583-1663)

In 1624, Ana became ruler of Ndongo, a state on the west coast of Africa. Her people were under attack on all sides. The Portuguese were raiding nearby villages in search of people they could kidnap as slaves, while the surrounding African kingdoms were closing in.

Ana knew she had to change something. She asked to meet with the Portuguese. Ana insisted on meeting them as equals. Although she knew that the Portuguese had brutally conquered various other parts of Africa, she wasn't ready to bow down to them. When she saw that the governor she was meeting with was sitting on the only chair in the room, she immediately told one of her assistants to get on her hands and knees and act as a chair for Ana so that she and the governor were equal.

To fend off the attacks, she made a treaty with Portugal and converted to Christianity.

But the Portuguese didn't keep up their side of the deal. Ana was forced to flee inland with her people. There, far from the reach of her enemies, Ana established a new state called Matamba.

To increase its power, she took in runaway slaves and Africans who had been forced to become soldiers by the Portuguese. Her fighting force was organized and young boys left their families and lived with their militia groups. It was a hard life but it was necessary for the people of Matamba to survive.

Ana lived to be eighty-one. By the time she died, Matamba was seen as an equal to the Portuguese colony. With her clever tactics and refusal to surrender, Ana had saved her people from a life of enslavement.

ANDREA BOCELLI

(BORN 1958)

Andrea had always had trouble with his eyesight but when a football collided with his head, it disappeared altogether. Doctors tried everything to get it back, even putting leeches into the eye sockets. Nothing worked. At twelve years old, Andrea had become completely blind.

That didn't stop him pursuing his passion. Andrea loved music more than anything. He played flute, saxophone, trombone, trumpet, guitar, drums, and piano. With his eyesight gone, he learned to read music written in Braille, so that he could keep learning and playing new pieces.

To keep his parents happy, Andrea went to university to become a lawyer. But it wasn't what he wanted to do. Instead, he studied with an Italian opera singer named Franco Corelli, and spent the evenings playing piano in bars to pay for the lessons. For years, this was Andrea's life.

Then, one day, the most famous opera singer in the world heard a recording of his voice.

The singer's name was Pavarotti and he knew he had to duet with Andrea. 'Miserere', the song they recorded together, was a hit, and Andrea's career finally began.

He's now sold over eighty million records, sung for three popes, and even had a beach in Italy named after him.

Andrea brought classical music from dusty practice halls to the top of the international music charts. He hopes more than anything that hearing his story might prove to young people there is no obstacle that can't be overcome.

'There is a project,' he says. 'That has been conceived for each of us.' It's just up to us to find that project.

ANANDI GOPAL JOSHI

(1865-1887)

As was common in nineteenth-century India, Anandi married when she was nine years old and gave birth to a child at the age of fourteen. Ten days later, the child died. Unfortunately, this was a frequent occurrence in India, where it was difficult to access any medical care at all.

Anandi was determined to change that.

At eighteen, she sailed across the ocean to America, where she applied at the Woman's Medical College of Pennsylvania. 'I may not have the qualifications you ask for,' she wrote in her application. 'But please give me a chance to help my poor suffering countrywomen.'

They accepted her and Anandi went on to graduate, becoming the first Indian woman to earn a degree in western medicine. Queen Victoria sent her a message of congratulations.

But all the time she had been studying, Anandi had been battling her own illness. She'd feel weak and out of breath, suffering headaches and fevers. The cold, damp climate of Pennsylvania was unfamiliar to her and it made her illness worse. Not long after returning home to Bombay, Anandi died. She was twenty-one years old.

Despite her life being cut short before Anandi was able to fulfil all her goals, she inspired a generation of women to break free of the roles they'd traditionally been assigned.

Several awards and fellowships in medicine have since been established in her name, and a gigantic crater on the planet Venus is named after her. On what would have been her 153rd birthday, Google changed their logo to a drawing of Anandi clutching her medical diploma. The world has not forgotten India's first female doctor.

CARNEGIE

ANDREW CARNEGIE

(1835-1919)

Andrew was twelve years old when he started work in a giant textile mill, dashing back and forth collecting bobbins of cotton. His family had sold everything they owned to move from Scotland to America in search of a better life. It was 1848 and Andrew earned $1.40 a week.

At fourteen, he got a job working as a secretary to a man called Thomas Scott, a secretary of the Pennsylvania Railroad Company. Andrew read and wrote and went to night school. A few years later, he had his boss's job.

While there, he invested in a company that made the first sleeper cars; train carriages where passengers could sleep peacefully as they chugged through the dusty American nights. They were a success and Andrew went to Europe in search of new investments.

On one trip, he met with steelmakers in England. Andrew could see great potential in the new metal because of its incredible strength and low cost. He headed back to America and set up his own steel plant.

Soon, he didn't just own steel plants, but the raw materials that were needed to make it, the ships and railroads to transport it, and the coal fields that provided fuel for the furnaces.

After selling his company, Andrew's net worth was around $475 million dollars, or $310 billion in today's money. He opened over 2800 libraries; set up trusts in the UK and America that would help students, children, and the poor; and created a peace foundation that sought to spread messages of harmony between nations.

Many of the trusts still run today. By the time he died, only around thirty million dollars of his fortune was left. 'A man who dies rich, dies disgraced,' Andrew wrote. He believed that there was no point in having money unless you used it to help others.

Today, Andrew's generosity continues to be felt by people all over the world.

ANDREA DUNBAR

(1961-1990)

Andrea grew up on the poor Buttershaw estate in Bradford, North England. It felt like living at the end of the world.

While she was still at school, Andrea fell pregnant, but the baby died. She was just fifteen. Drawing on her tragic life experiences, she wrote a play called *The Arbor* as part of an English final assignment. It told the story of a pregnant teenager struggling to live with an abusive father. Andrea went on to have three more children, the first when she was just seventeen.

While she was caring for her first child, Andrea carried on working on *The Arbor*. It was eventually sent to the Royal Court Theatre in London, where it caught the attention of a successful director. The play went on to be performed in London and New York, kicking up a flurry of attention, with Andrea at the centre of it all.

But Andrea struggled in the spotlight. The more success she found in London, the less she felt like she belonged back home in Bradford.

Once a film had been made of her second play, *Rita, Sue and Bob Too*, some of the residents on the Buttershaw estate felt Andrea was giving them a bad name. She tried not to care. 'If they are attacking me,' she said, 'they are leaving some other poor bugger alone.'

Andrea never moved away from Bradford, where she stayed and raised her kids. She would write once they were in bed and the housework had been done. Unfortunately, she died unexpectedly from a brain haemorrhage when she was only twenty-nine.

The Buttershaw estate has changed a lot since then, old buildings demolished and new homes built, but Andrea and her plays haven't been forgotten. They're still performed, turned into films, and written about now. Her writing remains a valuable window into the lives of the poorest and most overlooked members of society.

ANDY WARHOL

(1928-1987)

Thirty-two separate paintings of soup cans, copper metal turned blue with human pee, a bright yellow banana: these are all famous examples of work by Andy Warhol, one of the most ground-breaking artists who ever lived.

Andy grew up among the smog and grime of Pittsburgh, an industrial city in the east of America. He was ill as a child and forced to spend a lot of time in bed. To keep him from getting bored, his mother taught him how to sketch, paint, and print. Once he'd learned how, Andy never stopped.

Through a passion for art, he became the first person in his family to go to college. But he struggled, failing the first year. It looked like he wouldn't be allowed back.

That summer, Andy worked alongside his brother on a fruit and veg van. In quiet moments, he'd grab a pencil and sketch the strange characters who'd come to buy food. When a professor saw the drawings, Andy was allowed back to college, which he completed before boarding a train to New York City, determined to make it as an artist.

Andy would take familiar images and present them in ways no one had ever seen before. Like many other revolutionaries who had come before him, he tested the limits of what art could be. Marcel Duchamp had once put a toilet in an art gallery. Andy offered the world soap pads and coke bottles.

He also made experimental films, which people were confused by at the time but are now considered important. In one, a man eats a mushroom for forty-five minutes. In another, a poet sleeps for six hours.

Is it art?

Andy once claimed: 'Art is what you can get away with.'

When he died, Andy's will was fulfilled: his money was used to create The Andy Warhol Foundation. To this day, it encourages and promotes the risk-takers and mischief-makers of the art world.

ANNA AKHMATOVA

(1889-1966)

If you wrote a poem in the Soviet Union at the beginning of the twentieth century, you may have been putting yourself in terrible danger. The government, ruled by a brutal dictator named Stalin, might ransack your house, kidnap your relatives, and even make you disappear if you wrote anything that spoke against it.

Anna had been writing poetry since she was eleven. She'd never let anything stop her before. When her father said he didn't want his surname connected to her silly scribblings, she started using her grandmother's instead, and she moved away.

She travelled to St Petersburg and met a group of other young poets who shared the same ideas and hopes. They wrote together, creating their own movement and magazines, and soon the whole city was talking about them.

Then, when Stalin came to power, people started being taken away in the night, simply for talking out about the government. Expressing your opinion was forbidden.

Anna hated Stalin and his brutality. So the government filled her house with microphones, stationed spies outside to watch her, and threw the people she loved most into prison.

She was living in terror, and poetry was the only way she had of fighting back. But it had become too dangerous to write poems. Even if you wrote them down and hid them under your pillow, the police might search your house and find the evidence.

To get around this, Anna stopped writing her poems on paper. Instead, she created them in her head, then taught them to the women she could trust. She would recite them over and over again with her friends, until it was sure that someone would keep them safely in their memory.

Anna would not forget the people who had died and she didn't want the world to forget either.

'You will hear thunder and remember me,' she wrote.

After the Soviet Union collapsed, Anna became one of Russia's best loved poets.

CHRIS COLFER

(BORN 1990)

Stuck in a hospital bed for three months when he was a child, Chris Colfer would escape by reading his way into fictional worlds. He loved fairy tales most of all, anything that started with 'Once upon a time', and featured magic spells, evil witches, and heroic princesses.

At school, he never felt like he fitted in with the other kids. He once described himself as a llama. 'Where does a llama go?' he said. 'It's not a cow. It's not a horse.' He was bullied and felt alone.

Even if he couldn't find another llama, Chris at least found his passion: writing, acting, and singing. He performed at every opportunity. It hurt when the teachers at his school told him he couldn't sing one of his favourite songs, 'Defying Gravity', because it was supposed to be sung by a woman. His grandmother let him sing it in her church instead.

Once school was over, Chris auditioned for a part in a TV show called *Glee*. It followed a school choir that sings joyful covers of songs ranging from church hymns to pop hits.

Chris tried out for the role of Artie Abrams, a singer bound to a wheelchair because of a spinal cord injury in his youth. He didn't get the part. But the director of *Glee* was so impressed and invested in Chris's story that he wrote a character just for him.

The character was called Kurt Hummel. He was a gay student who loved clothes and singing in the *Glee* club, and found himself being bullied for both his passions and his sexuality. As the show took off, the writers included real stories from Chris's life, including an episode where his character was made fun of for singing 'Defying Gravity'.

Once the show had been a success, Chris went back to writing and immersed himself in the fictional worlds he'd visited as a child. The result was a novel called *The Land of Stories: The Wishing Spell*. In the story, a pair of twins are given a book that they realize is a portal between our world and the world of fairy tales.

Chris once said, 'You've got to show the world who you are before it tells you.'

BIDDY MASON

(1818-1891)

Biddy Mason was an African-American born into slavery. At a young age, she was torn away from her parents and sold repeatedly, from slaveowner to slaveowner. Eventually she ended up on the plantation of a man called Robert Smith, a Mormon living in Mississippi.

When church leaders put out the call for their followers to relocate to the west of America, Robert Smith set about moving his entire family and everything he owned. Over a gruelling two-thousand-mile trek, Biddy carried her youngest daughter on her back while she herded cattle, prepared meals, and looked after animals.

A few years later, Robert decided to move again, this time to California. While she was there, Biddy made friends with black people who weren't slaves, and who explained that California was a free state. While they were standing within that state's limits, no person was the property of another person. That made Robert Smith nervous, and he tried to escape with his slaves to Texas. But Biddy's friends went to the sheriff's office and a party rode out to stop Robert Smith before he could get away.

On January 19th 1856, Biddy earned freedom for herself and her extended family of thirteen.

She began work as a nurse, gaining a reputation for her encyclopaedic knowledge of herbal remedies. When patients couldn't pay, she gave her services for free. When they could, she saved every penny.

After ten years, Biddy bought two pieces of land and became the first black woman in Los Angeles to do so.

Biddy accumulated more and more wealth, always using it to help those around her. She fed the poor, let orphans live in her house, visited jails, and opened a school for black children.

'If you hold your hand closed,' Biddy said, 'nothing good can come in. The open hand is blessed, for it gives in abundance, even as it receives.'

Almost a hundred years after she died, November 16th was declared Biddy Mason Day in Los Angeles.

CHRIS PREDDIE

(BORN 1987)

For years, gang violence has been claiming the lives of young men on the streets of London. It has always surrounded Chris. In 2006, his cousins, Ricky and Danny, were convicted for killing a boy named Damilola Taylor, and his older brother was shot dead in a hairdresser's.

A youth worker asked Chris, is this the kind of life you want for yourself?

It wasn't. Chris knew he had to take the anger, the pain, and the sadness he felt over losing his brother, and use it as energy to turn his life around.

He went back to college and focused his efforts on studying music and drama. His teachers suggested he go into youth work and he did, hoping to change lives the way that one youth worker had helped change his.

Chris knows that most kids don't want to end up in gangs. Everyone wants a safe and comfortable life. Nobody wants to be afraid of walking the streets, afraid of ending up in jail, and afraid of being forced into dangerous situations. It's just sometimes gang life is the only path that seems available.

To help avoid this, Chris led a campaign through schools asking young people to call Crimestoppers with any information about gang activity. He wanted kids to know that it wasn't about snitching, but about saving lives. How would you feel if your own mother was hurt and no one would speak up?

In 2012, Chris got a letter in the post that he thought was a joke. The letter mentioned the queen and the prime minister and it invited him to Buckingham Palace to receive an Order of the British Empire. Chris became the youngest person ever to be honoured with an OBE. It was down to his role in trying to make the streets of London a safer place for those who walk them.

BIKINI KILL

(FORMED 1990)

Kathleen was always getting confused with Kathi at college because they both had shaved heads. Then Tobi started working in a sandwich shop on the same day as Kathi. And Billy met Tobi outside a Burger King before a punk show.

Together, the group formed Bikini Kill.

At the time, the punk music scene in Washington was dominated by male bands. It felt unwelcoming to girls. The music wasn't for them, the art wasn't for them, and the shows weren't for them. Bikini Kill wanted to know why it was that half of the world were women, suffering in ways particular to them, but no one was writing punk songs about it.

The band led the charge that changed that.

They headed a movement called Riot grrrl that fought to make space for women in punk rock. At shows, they encouraged their female fans to express themselves. They called for them to come up on stage to tell their stories. The band's song 'Rebel Girl' became an anthem for women of the Riot grrrl movement.

Tobi said she wanted to spread the message that all girls in all small towns across America should create bands and form their own culture.

And it worked.

Women made their own magazines, writing and illustrating them, then printing them off and stapling them together. More girl bands were born in garages, their demo tapes recorded in bedrooms.

Men were hostile. They claimed the band had no talent, and they threatened Kathleen, Kathi, Billy and Tobi. They assaulted them, even threatening to electrify the microphone and shock Kathleen, who was the singer.

'People hated us with a passion,' Kathleen said. But the young girls who came to their shows kept them going. For thousands of females who couldn't relate to the music being played on the radio, Bikini Kill were a source of energy and inspiration. They pushed aside the boys and made a space for feminism in underground music. Many bands today still thank Bikini Kill for leading the way.

CHRISTOPHER ROBIN

(1920-1996)

Growing up, Christopher Robin had three favourite toys: a bear, a donkey, and a pig. One day, when his nanny had to take some time off, Christopher was left alone with his father. The two of them decided to go exploring in the ancient woods that surrounded their cottage. They took Christopher's toys with them and spent hours making up stories of mischief and adventure.

Another day, the two of them went to visit a zoo, where they saw a huge black bear tumbling across the rocks in its enclosure.

'What's his name?' Christopher asked. 'Winnie,' his father told him.

Christopher decided to change the name of his bear. It would be called Winnie too, but not just Winnie, Winnie-the-Pooh.

Together with Christopher, his father made up more stories featuring the toys, and he wrote them down as a book. England had just come out of the First World War, so everyone was feeling gloomy, and happy tales of a greedy, honey-loving bear were exactly what was needed to cheer people up. The book was an instant bestseller.

But life changed for Christopher Robin. The games he'd played with his father were being read by the whole world and it felt as though nothing was private or his any more. At school, he was bullied for being the little boy in the stories. He was even pushed down the stairs one day. The whole world knew his name and it felt like everyone was taunting him.

When he got older, Christopher went to fight in the Second World War. He didn't want to be the character his father had written anymore, he wanted to be like everyone else. As a soldier he felt more normal. After he got back, he set up a bookshop and lived quietly above it with his wife. Instead of remaining the little boy in the stories, Christopher became his own person.

Christopher Robin's three toys, Piglet, Eeyore, and Winnie-the-Pooh, are now held in a glass case in New York Public Library where hundreds of thousands of people visit them every year.

BJÖRK

(BORN 1965)

Björk had always been very happy to be different. With her first pocket-money, she went out and bought a tent. She wanted to sleep outside. She wanted freedom and she found it among the vast, untouched highlands of Iceland.

She also found it through music. Björk had a voice that stood out. When she sang at her school, the song went on to be recorded, and she broke into the Icelandic charts at just eleven years old. Other children might have celebrated this. Not Björk. Stressed by the pressure, she stopped making music for a couple of years.

Then, when punk came to Iceland, Björk found an energy that excited her. She created an all-girl band called Spit and Snot and, when they split up, plenty more bands after that. At eighteen she travelled to England to play with one of them, even though she couldn't speak any English. She ended up sleeping in gardens.

After all the bands, Björk released her own music. Her unique voice, style, and indescribable, uncatchable, totally free songs set her apart from everyone else.

On one red carpet, she wore a dress shaped like a swan and pretended to lay an egg on the ground. She recorded an album in a cave filled with bats. In a music video, she slowly transformed into a polar bear.

After some difficult years, Björk created an album on her laptop, sitting alone with her headphones on, lost in swirling worlds of sound. The album was her biggest yet. But she still had to struggle with people thinking that men must have made the music for her, when really she had spent hours and hours stitching the notes together into shimmering melodies.

In 2000, the prime minister of Iceland tried to give Björk an island. She said no. She wanted to keep her privacy and her freedom.

Björk stayed true to herself.

CONSTANTIN BRÂNCUŞI

(1876-1957)

Constantin grew up in the tiny village of Hobita, Romania. His parents were poor peasant farmers and, from the age of seven, Constantin was expected to look after the sheep. He'd spend his time carving chunks of wood he found on the ground.

Constantin was always being bullied by his brothers and his father. He would run away from home but always ended up coming back. When he turned eleven, he escaped for good.

In the city of Craiova, Constantin survived by doing whatever jobs he could find. He worked as a grocer, as a fortune-teller, and serving drinks in a café. He also took a course in woodwork, to hone the skills he'd started learning as a child. Constantin made an entire violin out of scrap wood when he was eighteen years old. The feat was so impressive that a rich patron paid for Constantin to go and study at Romania's National School of Fine Arts in Bucharest. After he graduated, Constantin walked over two thousand kilometres to Paris.

There, he focused on sculpting.

Constantin carved by hand out of wood, stone, and metal. His creations were inspired by myths, folk tales, and the ways of ancient cultures. Most famous among them were his large, oval heads and sleek, shimmering birds in flight.

Constantin sculpted things the way they felt, not the way they looked.

Some critics said Constantin's sculptures were too abstract. He thought otherwise. To Constantin, what was most real about something was the idea or suggestion of it, not the accurateness of its appearance.

Once Romania became a communist country, Constantin never moved back, but he did try to leave his work to the government. They refused it.

Constantin became famous all over the world. Seventy years after they turned him down, the government are now trying to raise the eleven million dollars needed to buy a single piece by the boy-shepherd from Hobita.

CAROL BECKWITH

(BORN 1945)

& ANGELA FISHER

(BORN 1947)

Despite one being born in Australia and the other in America, both Carol Beckwith and Angela Fisher had always been drawn to Africa.

Carol first travelled there to visit a friend and ended up meeting with a group of Maasai people, a tribe of fierce warriors who move from place to place and centre their lives around cattle.

Angela had also fallen in love with the culture. She and Carol bonded immediately and set out together to photograph a Maasai warrior ceremony.

The two soon realized they shared a similar goal: to create a record of life on the vast, diverse continent that the very first humans came from.

Carol and Angela have since travelled over 270,000 miles, through forty countries, coming into contact with more than 150 different African cultures. They've made lifelong friends, been arrested, and witnessed great tides of change.

In Kenya, they met the Pokot people and saw the young girls of a tribe stand up against a traditional ritual that had been performed on women for hundreds of years. The ritual involves the girls being painfully and pointlessly mutilated for life. Not wanting to undergo the procedure, these girls left their tribe behind and moved into a missionary school, continuing to practise their culture with each other. Boys in another school learned of this and joined together with the girls, establishing a new group and banishing the painful, outdated tradition.

As wars rage, cities swell, and the modern world encroaches, traditions transform and disappear. Thanks to the photographs of Carol and Angela, these times of powerful and important change will not be forgotten.

DENG ADUT

(BORN 1980)

Deng grew up happily on his family's banana farm, in a fishing village beside the river Nile. One day, when he was six, everything changed.

War was raging in Sudan and the generals were desperate for conscripts. Soldiers arrived in Deng's village and dragged him away. For thirty-three days, he marched alongside thirty other children. Some boys were savaged by wild animals. Others were shot. And some boys just fell down dead, unable to carry on without food or water.

Deng made it to Ethiopia, where he was shown how to use an AK-47 and forced to fight for the Sudan People's Liberation Army. He was so small that the first time he fired the gun, it tore his arm out of its socket.

During the fighting, Deng saw and experienced unthinkable things, including children being blown up with grenades, and others dying from dehydration. Deng himself was severely wounded and almost bled to death.

Somehow he managed to reunite with his brother, John Mac. By hiding Deng under sacks on the back of a truck, John managed to smuggle him to Kenya. From there, the brothers secured passage to Australia, where they hoped to leave behind the brutality of war and start their lives again.

Deng has since studied law at university and become a defence lawyer. He now represents many of the Sudanese population in Australia, often for free.

In 2014, John Mac returned to Sudan to try to aid those still trapped there. He died while helping people escape across the river Nile. To make sure he's never forgotten, Deng has established a charity in his name. The John Mac Foundation aims to educate and empower people whose lives have been torn apart by war.

CHRISTINE DE PIZAN

(1364-1430)

Christine's father was the astrologer for King Charles V, which meant she could spend hours in the king's library, surrounded by books. She'd been born in 1364, a time when women weren't educated, but her father had insisted Christine was at least taught to read and write.

She loved to read but was horrified to see the kind of insulting things men had been writing about women. At the time, life for girls generally meant being bossed about by men, never owning anything, and not being allowed to hold any real jobs. Christine thought part of the reason women were being treated so badly was because they were being written about as though they were cruel or stupid creatures, rather than people.

When her father, and then her husband died, Christine was left alone with three young children to support, as well as her mother. She did the only thing she knew how to do: she wrote. Christine became the first female professional writer in France. By 1400, her poems of love and loss were being read around Europe.

But she also wanted to write about what it meant to be a woman. In *The Book of the City of Ladies*, Christine challenged people's ideas of what women were capable of by writing about strong and powerful women throughout history. She wrote about clearing the ground of old ideas and building a new city, one in which women are educated, respected, and allowed to assume useful roles in society.

Some scholars say Christine was writing some of the very first works of feminist literature in existence. After reading one of her letters, the French writer Simone de Beauvoir said that Christine's writing was 'the first time we see a woman take up her pen in defence of her sex.'

DOBRI DOBREV

(1914-2018)

Dobri was born in 1914, in a small Bulgarian village called Baylovo. He lost his father during the First World War and was raised by his mother. During attacks on Sofia in the Second World War, a bomb landed beside him and destroyed his hearing.

In 2000, Dobri gave everything he owned to the church and focused on living a life that brought good into the world. He moved into a small hut in the church courtyard and lived there until he died.

Every day he walked twenty kilometres into Sofia, the capital of Bulgaria, to sit outside the St Alexander Nevsky cathedral collecting money. What many people didn't realize was that every penny he collected, Dobri donated to churches, orphanages, and the poor. On one occasion, he gave over $20,000 to the cathedral he spent each day begging beside.

Sometimes people would ask what had happened in his life. Dobri would only say that he had once done something bad and was hoping to make up for it.

'The good will is just and true,' he said. 'We must love each other as God loves us.'

On the wall of an apartment building in Sofia, street artists painted a huge mural of Dobri holding a lit candle under his wise face. Newspapers called him 'The Living Saint of Baylovo'.

Dobri died at the age of 103. In a country struggling with poverty and corruption, he had become a symbol of true goodness and real hope.

DOROTHY DIETRICH

(BORN 1969)

The bullets were carried in by guards. One was chosen, loaded into a .22-calibre rifle, and aimed squarely at Dorothy's head. They were live on Canadian TV. She stood against a wall, wearing a red dress, with a metal cup clamped in her mouth. The gun fired.

Dorothy caught the bullet in her mouth.

In that moment, she became the first female magician to perform the famously dangerous bullet catch trick, a stunt that has killed numerous performers before and since.

She'd been escaping danger ever since she was a child. Playing cowboys with her brothers, Dorothy always ended up getting tied up. Somehow, she'd always manage to escape.

'Who do you think you are,' her aunt once said. 'Houdini?'

Dorothy went to the library to find out who Houdini was. She read that he'd been an escapologist who had amazed the world by freeing himself from chains, dangling upside down from skyscrapers, and surviving being buried alive.

Dorothy wanted to do the same. She left home at thirteen and hitchhiked to New York City to be a magician.

It felt as though she was following in her hero's footsteps, as Houdini had run away at twelve to join the circus.

She studied her art and learned everything she could about it from books and living magicians. Soon, Dorothy was performing in hotels, schools, and nightclubs. Her routines became famous. They featured two poodles, a duck, doves, coins being plucked from the air, and audience members being made to float above the stage.

When Dorothy was invited to perform on TV, she wanted to change how things were done. Why did it always have to be men sawing women in half? She sawed in half any celebrity who would let her.

Now Dorothy owns a museum dedicated to her hero, Harry Houdini, and she performs there whenever she can.

DR SEUSS

(1904-1991)

Theodor Seuss's father owned a brewery that produced over 300,000 barrels of beer every year. Unfortunately for him, the American government banned alcohol in 1920, and the brewery was forced to close.

Instead, he was put in charge of the parks in the area, which included Springfield Zoo. Often he would take Theodor there to observe the animals, and Theodor would bring along his sketchpad. With the encouragement of his mother, he filled the walls of his bedroom with drawings, while she made up rhymes about pie flavours to make him laugh.

Theodor went to college at Dartmouth, where he made his closest friends and worked tirelessly on the school's humour magazine. Whenever they shook hands, Theodor and his friends would jokingly say, 'Oh, the places you'll go! The people you'll meet!'

As the Second World War plunged the world into darkness, Theodor joined the army as part of Frank Capra's wartime film-making unit. They were tasked with raising the spirits of the troops and of the people waiting back home.

The war ended and Theodor moved to California. After finding out how many American kids were struggling to learn how to read, Theodor wanted to help. He knew the books they used in schools could be boring and he wanted to create something fun that children actually enjoyed reading.

The result was *The Cat in the Hat*, which Theodor published under the name Dr Seuss. The book is a bizarre rhyming tale that captivated millions of children, teaching them how to read, while making them fall about laughing at the same time.

Under the name Dr Seuss, Theodor went on to write many books that introduced kids to the thrill of reading, including *Green Eggs and Ham*, *Horton Hears a Who!*, and *The Grinch Who Stole Christmas*.

Oh, the Places You'll Go! was the last book he wrote before he died. His stories are still read with delight by kids and parents everywhere.

ELIZABETH OF HUNGARY

(1207-1231)

Elizabeth was born in 1207, the daughter of King Andrew of Hungary. At fourteen, she was married to an aristocrat named Ludwig of Thuringia, whom she grew to love deeply and had three children with.

It was always important to her to live by the principles of the Gospel. Where others could have chosen to live a relaxed life of pleasure and luxury, Elizabeth focused her efforts on helping those less fortunate than herself.

While Ludwig was away on business, floods washed over the land of Thuringia. Elizabeth built a hospital and helped everyone she could, even when it meant giving away clothes or objects from the royal house. She wore simple clothes rather than the grand finery of the rich and would stand at the gates of her castle, handing out bread to the poor.

Ludwig died while on crusade to Jerusalem. Heartbroken, Elizabeth swore she would never remarry.

Ludwig's family looked down on her for giving so much away to the poor and they threw her out of the home she had once shared with her husband. Her children were sent away because she no longer had the means to care for them.

Elizabeth put all of her remaining money into another hospital where she herself walked among the beds, tending sick patients.

She died in November 1231. It was said that miracles began occurring on her grave. Blind children were made to see, the lame were made to walk, and the dead were even resurrected to life. Four years after her death, Elizabeth was made a saint.

THE EDELWEISS PIRATES

During the brutal Nazi reign of Germany, many children joined the Hitler Youth, an organization meant to teach them hate and cruelty. By 1936, all ten- to eighteen-year-olds were told they had to join, or face severe punishments.

But not everyone did.

The Edelweiss Pirates were groups of young people across Germany who resisted the Nazis by refusing to join the Hitler Youth. The Pirates tended to be working-class teenagers between the ages of fourteen and seventeen years old, with jobs in factories and mills. They felt stifled by the control the Nazis had over people's lives. Jazz music had been banned, thousands of books were burned, and people were afraid of having honest conversations about the oppressive regime in case someone overheard and reported them.

In the hills and fields of Germany, the Pirates found the freedom to say and sing what they wanted. They would take hikes through the countryside, sleeping in barns and tents, and sing folk songs around campfires. They wore long hair, checkered shirts, lederhosen, and neck scarves. They scrawled 'Down With Hitler' on the walls of their cities.

If they came across deserters from the army or prisoners escaped from camps, the Pirates would shelter them in their homes. Every time they walked past a car belonging to a Nazi, they poured sugar into the petrol tank. They would have street battles with the Hitler Youth, raid Nazi supply stores, and organize campaigns to spread information to the allies – a group of countries who were opposed to the Nazis – however possible.

It was a dangerous group to be involved with. Pirates who were caught could be beaten, sent away to concentration camps, or even hanged. Still, they met and they sang:

Hitler's power may lay us low,
And keep us locked in chains,
But we will smash the chains one day,
We'll be free again.

ELLEN MacARTHUR

(BORN 1976)

In the book *Swallows and Amazons*, two families of children spend a summer sailing their boats around a lake, camping under the stars, and fishing for their dinner. As she lay in bed reading it, Ellen dreamed of one day captaining her own boat.

She saved her school-dinner money for three years, until finally buying her first dinghy. It was named *Threp'ny Bit*, after an old British coin that used to be worth one eightieth of a pound.

When she was eighteen, Ellen sailed around the whole of Britain. She was hooked and started racing in competitions that spanned the globe.

After several failed attempts, she tried to break the world record for fastest solo around the world journey. Ellen sailed non-stop for twenty-four hours a day, never sleeping for longer than twenty minutes at a time.

But she had support.

The British public cheered her on from their living rooms, following her progress through video diaries recorded as her boat was thrown mercilessly about by fifty-foot waves.

Ellen broke the record, completing the trip in seventy-one days, fourteen hours, eighteen minutes, and thirty-three seconds. Her voyage made her famous and Ellen wanted to do something useful with her fame.

She'd had a lot of time to think while she was sailing alone. She thought about how people had once hunted whales until there were almost none left. She thought about how, unless something changes, by 2050 there will be more plastic in the ocean than fish. She realized that unless we changed the way we were doing things, we were going to use up everything on our planet.

It hurt but she decided to walk away from racing to set up her own charity. The Ellen MacArthur Foundation aims to shift the world towards a more sustainable way of living. Hopefully, it will help preserve the ocean for future generations of young sailors.

ELLEN CRAFT

(1826-1891)

& WILLIAM CRAFT

(1824-1900)

Ellen and William were married slaves who belonged to different owners in Macon, Georgia. As Ellen's father was white, she was born light-skinned. So light-skinned that she was often confused for a member of the slaveowner's family.

This gave William an idea. Some of the states in America were free states. If you could make it to one of them, you would no longer be a slave. But two slaves travelling together to one of those places would be captured, sent back, and beaten. A slaveowner and his slave, however, could travel far more easily.

William cut Ellen's hair short. She put on men's trousers that she had sewed herself, glasses and a top hat. Lastly, they put her arm in a sling, so she wouldn't be asked to read and sign anything.

The couple snuck away from their plantations and headed for Macon train station, where they bought tickets for Savannah, a town two hundred miles away. While William rode in the slaves' carriage, Ellen sat nervously between two gentlemen in a separate carriage and pretended to be deaf. From Savannah, the Crafts caught a steamboat to Philadelphia, one of the free states. Their journey had lasted four days.

On their first day of freedom, William and Ellen received their first reading lesson. They eventually settled in Boston, where William became a cabinetmaker and Ellen a seamstress.

Two years later, a slave hunter came looking for William and Ellen. They fled to England. For nineteen years, they lived in Surrey.

Slavery was formally abolished in 1865. Three years later, the Crafts returned to America and set up a farm school for newly freed slaves.

EMMA GONZÁLEZ

(BORN 1999)

Every year, over thirty thousand people in America are killed by guns. In the United Kingdom, the number is around fifty. Guns are legal to buy and own in most states of America. In the United Kingdom, guns are illegal.

On 14th February 2018, an ex-student stormed into Emma González's school with a semi-automatic rifle and killed seventeen people, most of them students. It was the 208th school shooting in America since 1999.

It left Emma and her classmates traumatized. They had been trapped for two terrifying hours in their own school hall, fearing for their lives.

As the students mourned for their lost friends, they also called out for change. Why are guns so easy to get hold of? they asked. Why are they legal when they aren't making thing safer? Who is going to help us achieve change?

They joined a fight that had been raging for years. While some Americans desire the freedom to own guns, others demand the right to live in a society that's free of them. Emma captured America's attention. She made stirring speeches and heartfelt pleas to the lawmakers of her country, asking for stricter gun laws. On behalf of her lost friends, she demanded change.

Before the tragedy, Emma had been a student who enjoyed art, astronomy and writing, led her school's gay-straight alliance, and shaved her head to keep cool in the Florida heat. After the tragedy, she became the most visible anti-gun campaigner in the world.

Emma organized March For Our Lives, a peaceful protest event that took place on 24th March, in support of new gun control laws. Between 1.3 and 2 million people took part, making it the largest student protest in American history.

'After all of this pain and all of this death caused by gun violence,' Emma said, 'it seems as if the kids are the only ones who still have the energy to make change.'

I WILL VOTE
WE CALL B.S.
PEACE
MARCH FOR OUR

ERIC UNDERWOOD

(BORN 1984)

Eric first learned to dance with his sisters. As the radio played pop music, they'd have street dance contests outside their house in suburban Maryland. But it was a dangerous neighbourhood. When gunshots echoed through the streets, his mother would make Eric and his sisters drop to the floor.

One day his mum made Eric go to an acting audition at a performing arts school. It didn't go well. Eric found himself forgetting all the lines he'd rehearsed.

'Is there anything else you might be suited to?' the teachers asked. Eric quickly realized he wouldn't get a place if he didn't think of something. Through an open door, he glimpsed a group of girls limbering up before a ballet lesson.

'I'll try that,' he said, uncertainly.

They gave him a trial and soon Eric was taking regular classes, spending hours going to different parts of the city to train.

Eric would watch videos of famous ballets on YouTube, over and over, trying to master the moves. He'd balance his legs on his bunk bed to stretch.

At fifteen, he won a scholarship to the School of American Ballet.

Sometimes Eric was treated differently because he was black, whereas ballet traditionally attracted white people. Ballet shoes had always been light pink, to disguise them against pale skin and, as no shoes for black dancers existed, Eric had to cover his in dark make-up before every show.

Despite that, Eric has gone on to become the star of The Royal Ballet in London. Thanks to him, a company have finally released a ballet shoe for people with darker skin. It's called Eric Tan.

When he visited a boys' school, Eric met two kids that had clear talent. One of the boys was encouraged by his parents and went on to train. The other was told by his dad that he had to play football instead. That upset Eric.

He wants people to realize that ballet is for everyone: rich and poor, men and women, young and old. It's just another way of expressing yourself, and of entertaining the world.

EVONNE GOOLAGONG CAWLEY

(BORN 1951)

As a child, Evonne would spend hours and hours hitting a ball against a water tank with a piece of wood. She was told to join the tennis club and she did, signing up with a coach and even moving in with his family.

Evonne is a Wiradjuri Indigenous Australian. Her people had lived in Australia for thousands of years before white settlers arrived from England, taking their lands and killing them, until their numbers dwindled and their lives were uprooted.

The Indigenous Australian people believe that everything in existence – from rivers to mountains and people to kangaroos – was created by their ancestors during the Dreaming, at the very beginning of everything. They play music using didgeridoos and clapsticks, two of the oldest musical instruments ever to be invented, and create intricate artworks, once on the walls of caves or rock, now in an array of different ways.

Despite the legacy of discrimination that faces Indigenous Australians in modern Australia, Evonne triumphed as an athlete representing the Wiradjuri Nation and Australia.

She moved to America and excelled at tennis, being crowned the number one player in the world on two occasions. She won fourteen Grand Slams, was named Australian of the Year, and even had her face appear on a postage stamp. For nine years, she was ranked in the top ten players in the world. She became only the second woman ever to win Wimbledon as a mother.

After her own mother died, Evonne went home to Australia, wanting to explore her Indigenous Australian heritage. She set up the Evonne Goolagong Foundation, which aims to use tennis camps as a way of improving education, health, and create opportunities for Indigenous Australian kids. For twenty-two years now, the foundation has helped kids achieve their potential, just the way Evonne did.

EUGENE HÜTZ

(BORN 1972)

In 1986, the Chernobyl nuclear power plant exploded, releasing radioactive particles into the air of the Ukraine. Eugene was thirteen. His family fled Kiev to live with his grandmother, a Romany gypsy who had settled in the city. Traditionally the gypsies had lived nomadic lifestyles, always travelling, but that had been made illegal and so most had been forced into apartment blocks and government jobs.

After some time, Eugene's family moved between camps for asylum seekers in Poland, Austria, and Italy. They eventually settled in Burlington, Vermont in America. It was impossible to go back to Kiev, as Eugene's father was being threatened by the Soviet government, who was suspicious of the rock band in which he played the guitar.

Eugene's father passed on his love of music, taking him to see punk rock bands and teaching him to play a guitar they built together out of scrap wood.

When Eugene got older, he moved to New York, where he met a group of other immigrants from all over the world who were obsessed with gypsy music, either through their roots or their passion. Together they formed a band called Gogol Bordello. They played loud, raucous music, influenced by gypsy, folk, rock, punk, and the nationalities of everyone in the band. Sergey from Russia played violin, Tommy from Ethiopia played bass, Pedro from Ecuador rapped, Ori from Israel played saxophone, and huge numbers of other musicians from all walks of life have jammed with the band.

Their first big album was called *Gypsy Punks: Underdog World Strike*.

On his yearly trip back to the gypsy camps of the Ukraine, Eugene played it to some Romany people. They laughed, not knowing what to make of their traditional melodies being played with electric guitars and computer drum machines.

In an America divided by prejudice, Eugene's wild and joyful celebrations of immigration and international friendship are more important than ever.

GERTRUDE STEIN

(1874-1946)

In the early 1900s, writers and artists from all over the world were flocking to Paris. They painted gloomy pictures of rain-slicked streets, composed romantic poems by the river Seine, and wrote novels recording their escapades.

At the centre of it all was Gertrude.

She'd been born in America, but grew up travelling between countries with her parents. When they finally settled in California, Gertrude found school unchallenging and spent most of her time reading.

Eventually she went on to study medicine at university. It didn't go well. Medicine at the time was dominated by men and Gertrude was always getting into arguments with men who thought they knew better than her. Discouraged, she quit without earning her degree, and moved to Paris to be with her brother.

The two of them collected art together. They filled the house they shared with oil paintings and sculptures. By 1906, their art collection featured pieces that would go on to become some of the most famous in the world, including paintings by Cézanne, Matisse, and Picasso. Those painters also became some of Gertrude's closest friends.

Every Saturday night, her house would fill with poets, artists, and writers, all keen to gather around Gertrude to ask her advice, soak up her wisdom, and hear her stories. From Hemingway to Picasso, Fitzgerald to Matisse, everyone wanted to spend Saturdays at 27 rue de Fleurus, celebrating life, art, and the thrill of being around creative people.

Gertrude also wrote, and she did it like no one else. Some people thought it was nonsense, but other people thought her work was the most beautiful thing they'd ever read.

In *Tender Buttons*, she wrote: 'Asparagus in a lean in a lean to hot. This makes it art and it is wet wet weather wet weather wet.'

By gathering struggling artists under her wing and pushing the limits of language, Gertrude single-handedly helped drag art into the twentieth century.

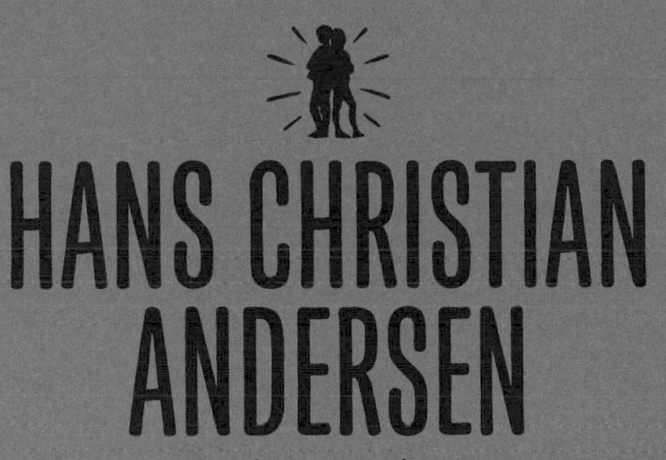

HANS CHRISTIAN ANDERSEN

(1805-1875)

You may have heard the story of the princess and the pea. You may also have heard the story of the naked emperor, convinced he's wearing a marvellous coat, and the story of the little mermaid, who dwells in an underwater kingdom but longs to walk among humans on the land. All these stories were written by Hans Christian Andersen.

Hans was born in Denmark. His mother was a washerwoman who couldn't read or write and his father was a shoemaker who told bedtime stories. They quickly became Hans's passion. Trapped with his parents in a one-roomed house, he escaped through tales inside his own head.

At fourteen, he left home for Copenhagen, the capital of Denmark. He did well at first, getting a part in a choir that made good money. Then, when Hans got older, his voice broke and he was kicked out. Next he tried to be a ballet dancer but found he was clumsy and couldn't control his arms and legs. Finally Hans tried manual labour, quickly realizing he wasn't meant for that, either.

Then he had a piece of luck. Hans met a man called Jonas Collin, who was impressed by the stories he'd been writing. Jonas convinced the king of Denmark to pay for Hans to be educated.

School was one of the darkest times of Hans's life. He was picked on by the other children and beaten by his schoolmaster. Again, he escaped into his stories. Once he graduated, he committed himself to writing.

His fairy tales went unnoticed until *The Little Mermaid*. With that story, Hans was launched into the global spotlight. His stories continue to be told today, on screens, in books, and by parents all over the world.

GRETA GERWIG

(BORN 1983)

Growing up at a Catholic school in Sacramento, California, Greta always felt like everything was happening somewhere else. She danced ballet and fenced, though acting was always her real passion. Wearing red converse shoes and glasses while playing Dorothy in *The Wizard of Oz*, she dreamed of moving to New York to become an actress.

Unfortunately, the acting schools she applied for didn't accept her. Still, she moved to New York and studied English and Philosophy. At least she was escaping Sacramento for somewhere more exciting.

She found a way to make films, too. Instead of auditioning for parts in big movies, Greta made her own with her friends. The films all had certain things in common: they were filmed on cheap cameras, mostly improvised, and generally just featured people talking to each other.

They got Greta noticed, and she went on to be cast in bigger and bigger productions.

As she rose to fame, Greta began missing the grand old houses, tree-lined avenues, and winding rivers of her hometown. She wanted to go back and she wanted to make a film there. Not just star in one, but write it and direct it.

Greta did make her own film, about a girl at a Catholic school in Sacramento. The film was called *Lady Bird*, and followed a teenager who dyes her hair pink, changes her name, and spends her days dreaming of escaping her sleepy town for a big city.

Over a year later, at 5.22 in the morning, Greta woke up, made coffee, and checked her phone. *Lady Bird* had been nominated for an Oscar. In over ninety years of Academy Awards, Greta was only the fifth woman to ever be nominated for the award. She cried, laughed, and shouted. Hopefully, she thinks, it will inspire a new generation of young women to get out and make their own films.

GRETA

HERMETO PASCOAL

(BORN 1936)

Hermeto was born albino, which means there's no colour pigment in his skin and he has difficulty seeing. Growing up in the countryside of Brazil, he couldn't work in the fields with his family as the fierce sun would burn his pale skin. Instead, he stayed indoors and taught himself how to play music. His family lived in a poor area with no special education available for Hermeto, who needed extra help to see. He dropped out of school when he was ten and devoted his life to music.

When he was old enough, Hermeto moved to Rio de Janeiro, where the statue Christ the Redeemer kept watch over the city and the Copacabana beach twinkled blue as the sun set.

There, he made music out of everything within reach: glasses, tables, body parts, animals. To Hermeto, everything was an instrument. Everything in the world held within it the possibility of music.

It was music recorded in Rio de Janeiro that caught the attention of Miles Davis, one of the most famous jazz musicians on the planet. Miles was astonished by Hermeto. He thought he was one of the most talented musicians in the world and insisted on recording songs with him.

Hermeto's career took off after that, and he now tours across the globe with his band. There is no one else making music like him. Hermeto doesn't stick to genres, like classical or jazz, he plays whatever comes to him.

Thanks to a childhood in the countryside, Hermeto is often inspired by nature and tries to incorporate it into his melodies. In one composition, 'Música da Lagoa', musicians burble underwater in a lagoon, while flautists stand playing in the water.

He's since moved back to the area where he was born. Hermeto spends his days hosting musicians, spending time with his family, and letting the music flow through him.

HANNAH HERBST

(BORN 2000)

One day, Hannah received a letter from her nine-year-old penpal, Ruth, who lived in Ethiopia, on the east coast of Africa. Ruth wrote about how her family struggled without electricity or clean drinking water. Hannah lived in Florida, America, and she couldn't imagine life without water running from the taps and lights on at night. She wanted to help.

She had been interested in science ever since going to an engineering camp when she was eleven. At the camp, she'd realized she was the only girl. It made her feel nervous and lonely, but the thrill of programming robots convinced her to stay.

Hannah wanted to channel her passion for science into doing something that might help Ruth. She created plans for a small machine called BEACON, which stands for Bringing Electricity Access to Countries through Ocean Energy. The device would float in a body of water and use the movement of the waves to generate electricity, which could then be used to clean water and power homes.

Her first model kept breaking, over and over. It frustrated Hannah but she didn't give up, just learned from every failure and carried on making tweaks until her idea became reality.

The invention won her the title of America's Top Young Scientist. She was only fourteen. Prize money and time with a leading scientist meant she could continue improving the design of her machine. She was flown to Switzerland, where Hannah tested newer versions of BEACON on glassy green lakes. She even visited the White House to discuss her views on how we can best help those in need.

At sixteen, Hannah enrolled at Florida Atlantic University to study computer engineering. She's still at work on BEACON. When it's ready, she's not going to sell it, but open-source it, which will mean that people all around the world, including Ruth, can build it for free using her plans.

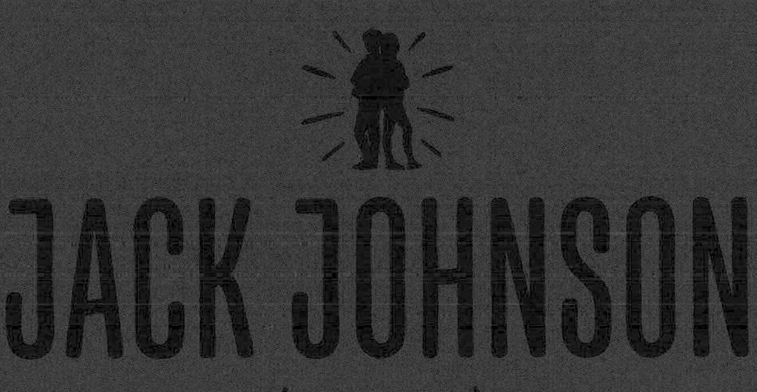

JACK JOHNSON

(BORN 1975)

Jack grew up in Hawaii, between pineapple fields and golden beaches. He started surfing soon after he started walking. At seventeen, he became the youngest ever person to be invited to surf in the Pipeline Masters, one of the islands' biggest competitions.

But an accident cut his surfing career short. Jack fell and smacked his head on the reef, needing 150 stitches and losing a handful of teeth. It didn't end his love of surfing, though it did mean he had to slow down.

He made surfing videos with his friends and recorded the music to them himself. Soon people were asking for tapes of the music. His first album, *Brushfire Fairytales*, was a collection of songs he'd written and played for his friends around campfires on the beach. It sold over a million copies.

His third album, *In Between Dreams*, sold fifteen million. It was gentle, happy music, that relaxed people and brought smiles to their faces. At a time when economies everywhere were beginning to crash, Jack's music offered a little bit of peace.

He embarked on tours to play around the world and donated one hundred per cent of all profits to charity. After every show, some of the money was given away to local organizations that looked after the environment, and the rest was put into a foundation aimed at promoting alternatives to plastic, sustainable local food, and other hands-on environmental projects.

'Love is when you find that thing,' Jack says, 'when you want to give more than you want to take.'

Jack still tries to surf every day, waking up before his kids so he has time to catch a few waves. Being out on the ocean is the easiest way to make himself feel alive.

HUA MULAN

Thousands of years ago, vicious tribes from the north were wreaking havoc across China and the emperor was calling on every household to provide fighters for the army. Seeing the soldiers approach her village for recruits, Mulan was afraid. Her father was old and she knew he wouldn't survive a war.

She charged back to the house, cut off her hair, and dressed herself up as a boy. When the soldiers came to the door, Mulan presented herself as her father's son, and offered to go and fight in the war.

After twelve years in the mud and stink of battle, Mulan was promoted to the rank of general. She also fell in love with an officer who fought beside her, Jin Yong. When Mulan told Jin Yong she was a woman, he fell deeply in love with her too. He promised to keep her secret safe.

As the war drew to a close, and the marauding tribes had been conquered, the emperor of China offered Mulan an official position and bountiful rewards for her heroism. Mulan refused. She only asked for a horse so that she could return home to her family and a couple of soldiers to accompany her on the journey.

Her father squinted into the sun as Mulan approached their village. Who was this grand and powerful general? he thought to himself. Realizing it was his daughter, he was overjoyed.

In the safety of her home, Mulan took off her armour and put on the clothes she'd dressed in before joining the army. The two soldiers who'd escorted her back were astounded. The whole time, their fearless general had been a woman.

The story of Mulan went on to be recorded in songs that were sung all across China. Over a thousand years later, her tale was made into a Disney film: *Mulan*.

JOHN BRADBURNE

(1921-1979)

John Bradburne was born to a normal family in Cumbria, England. He had to put his studies on hold when war broke out in 1939.

During the war, he served with the Gurkhas: soldiers from Nepal who were recruited into the British army. He defended Singapore, living for months in a jungle when it fell, and was then shipwrecked while trying to escape. This caused him to have a religious experience.

Back in England, John stayed for a while with an order of monks, before setting out on his travels through France, Italy, Greece, Turkey, and Egypt. Then John found the place where he felt his help was needed most.

Mutemwa is a leper colony in Zimbabwe, a country in southern Africa. The inhabitants of Mutemwa all suffer from a disease called leprosy, which can cause sight loss, nerve damage, and the loss of fingers, toes, hands, and feet. In the past, people believed that leprosy was contagious. Even though we know today that isn't true, many people suffering from the condition are still forced to live separate to everyone else.

John found the people in Mutemwa starving, dirty, and living in ramshackle huts. He moved in alongside them. John clipped nails, chased away rats, brought food, sang songs, and fixed up buildings. He did everything he could to improve the lives of the people in Mutemwa.

One day the association that ran Mutemwa kicked John out. Why? Because he didn't like the people who lived there being known by numbers, so he gave them all names, and he insisted that everyone was given at least a loaf of bread a week.

John wouldn't leave the people he'd promised to help. For the rest of his days, he lived on a nearby mountain, travelling down every day to help the residents of Mutemwa.

Pilgrims still travel to John's shrine at Mutemwa and a charity started in his name continues to look after people suffering from leprosy. It's hoped that the Church will soon declare him a saint.

INDIRA RANAMAGAR

(BORN 1970)

When adults in Nepal are sentenced to prison, they often have to bring their young children in with them. Conditions in the jails are dirty, cramped and dangerous. Children who live in them aren't given medical care, proper food, education, or any chance of a real childhood.

Seeing this, Indira wanted to make a difference.

Indira was born into poverty and forbidden from going to school with her brothers, since she was a girl. Instead, she taught herself to write by scratching letters into the dirt with a stick and absorbing everything she could from her brothers' textbooks. She did finally make it into the village school. She came out top of the class.

Indira went on to become a schoolteacher and provided reading lessons for the women of her village. Still, she felt like she could be doing more. So she travelled to Kathmandu, the capital of Nepal, where she met a human rights activist called Parijat, who showed her what life was like in the prisons. Many of the people locked away were put there for tiny crimes, like stealing food when they were starving, and many others were mentally ill.

To help, Indira founded Prisoner's Assistance Nepal, to care for the children who have parents in jail. She opened four children's homes and two schools. Since then, Indira has rescued over 1600 children and currently has around five hundred under her care.

She continues her work with the solemn determination of that child who once stood scratching the alphabet into the dirt.

'Every child should have a right to live with dignity,' Indira said. 'That's my fighting, that's my dream.'

JOHN BOYEGA

(BORN 1992)

John was in the bottom set for every subject at school. He wasn't interested in sports either. All he wanted to do was daydream about his favourite films, like *Star Wars*, and the parts he would one day play in them.

The first time he'd acted was as a leopard in his school play. After that, he knew performing was what he wanted to do. He enrolled in a local theatre school to learn ballet, tap, and modern dance. It didn't make him popular on his estate in Peckham. Kids would pick on him for being different. His dad tried to get involved but there was nothing he could do.

While still at school, John got a role in a film called *Attack the Block*, about a group of teenagers living on an estate in London who have to defend themselves when aliens attack.

Because of his captivating performance, John was cast as the first black Stormtrooper in the new incarnation of *Star Wars*. His character, Finn, leaves the First Order after realizing they're evil, and sides with the resistance in the fight to gain control of the galaxy. Alongside Rey, Han Solo, and Chewbacca, he flies the Millennium Falcon to the ice planet, Starkiller Base.

When the trailer came out, there was a fuss. Why? Because John is black. Some people spoke out against the idea of a black Stormtrooper for no reason other than sheer racism. 'To whom it may concern,' John wrote. 'Get used to it.' He said most people were excited. And it showed. The film made a billion dollars in twelve days.

When he got his first cheque, John told his parents they had to come and do an interview about him. He gave them the address of where the interview was. They turned up at a beautiful house – the kind his dad had always dreamed of – with white walls and wooden floors.

'What does it feel like to have the best son in the world?' John asked. He'd moved them out of the small flat they'd rented their entire lives, and he'd bought them a house.

John's daydreams were coming true.

IRENA SENDLER

(1910-2008)

In 1999, four students in Kansas, America, were handed an old newspaper clipping about a woman called Irena Sendler. When they Googled her, they found only one result. They were determined to find out more. This is what they learned:

When the Nazis took control of Warsaw in World War Two, they forced all of the Jews living there to move to one tiny area, called a ghetto, that was sealed off from the rest of the city by a ten foot fence. Life in the ghetto was unbearable. Children starved to death, people died from cold, and disease spread rapidly through the overcrowded population.

Irena was horrified and joined Zegota, a secret underground group dedicated to helping Jewish people. She was a nurse and used her position to sneak medical supplies and food into the ghetto, and to smuggle children out of it. She hid them in ambulances, led them through the sewer system, and even concealed them in sacks and suitcases, risking her own life in the process.

Ultimately, Irena saved 2,500 children, rehoming them under new names so that the Nazis could never find them. She wrote the real identities of the children on pieces of paper and buried them in jars under an apple orchard in her neighbour's garden. She hoped one day to be able to dig up the jars and tell the children who they really were.

Irena was eventually arrested and tortured for information on Zegota. Her legs and feet were broken but she refused to talk and was sentenced to be shot. Posters put up around the city announced that she had been killed. They were untrue. The rebel group had bribed the guard and had Irena taken to safety.

Once the war was over, she dug up the jars and tried to help the children find their families. Sadly, many of the children's relatives had died at the hands of the Nazis.

The four students in Kansas wrote a play called *Life in a Jar* to let the world know the bravery of Irena Sendler. If you Google her today, you'll find over 500,000 results.

DJ
FOCUS

KELVIN DOE

(BORN 1996)

Kelvin was born in one of the poorest areas of Freetown, the capital city of Sierra Leone. The electricity in his neighbourhood was so unreliable that the lights would only come on once a week.

From the age of ten, Kelvin would spend his afternoons after school scouring rubbish dumps for old electronics. He would carefully take apart the devices to figure out how they worked and then piece them back together in inventions that came straight out of his own mind. His mother would get home to find the house looking like a tip, with circuit boards and wires strewn across the floor.

'Why do you have to go digging around in bins?' she'd ask.

Working on the living room floor, Kelvin made batteries for power lamps, generators to make electricity when it wasn't available, sound mixers, and even a radio transmitter, which he used to broadcast his own radio station. Kelvin used the name DJ Focus because he believes that with focus, anyone can achieve what they set out to do.

And Kelvin's focus and creativity were soon noticed. He was interviewed on local TV and a man called David Sengeh invited him to visit one of the most prestigious engineering universities in America. There, Kelvin recorded an inspirational talk that was seen by millions of people.

'Creativity is universal,' Kelvin said in his speech, 'and can be found in places where one does not expect to find it.'

Since then, Kelvin has moved to Canada and started his own company. Their first product is a solar-powered light and phone charger that can run for thirty hours. He spends the rest of his time working for a group that offers help to the victims of war and poverty.

JAMIE CHADWICK

(BORN 1998)

On August 24th 2015, Jamie Chadwick won the British GT Championship, driving an Aston Martin V8 Vantage. The next morning, she put on her uniform and went to school. At seventeen, Jamie was the youngest ever winner and the first female to win the prestigious race.

Jamie started racing go-karts when she was thirteen. That led her to the Ginetta Junior Scholarship, where drivers are eliminated until only the winners remain. From there she earned a place at Aston Martin's racing academy.

Racing is a predominantly male sport. Jamie says men make jokes about her being a woman driver but she doesn't listen. Since winning the British GT Championship, she's been racing in Formula Three, where the average top speed of the cars is 270 kmh. Now she's dreaming about taking part in Formula One. No woman has raced in Formula One since Lella Lombardi in 1976 and Jamie's hoping to be next. When one of the heads of Formula One claimed that women aren't capable of driving the cars, Jamie knew what he was saying was nonsense and became even more determined to prove him wrong. If she gets there, she'll be zooming around the track at over 350 kmh.

One of the biggest obstacles in racing is the cost. Most drivers come from wealthy families with spare money to pump into their careers. Although she has some sponsors, Jamie has to save every penny she can.

It's also very demanding physically. Drivers have to train hard, since they move at such speeds that extremely strong G-force acts on their bodies, the same as for astronauts. Now Jamie trains in racing gyms but she used to have to make her helmet extremely heavy, and lie on her bed with her head hanging off until her neck gave up.

Her coaches think she has what it takes. 'She is an out and out racer,' said one.

Jamie's showing everyone that being a girl makes absolutely no difference to how fast she can tear around a racetrack.

KESZ VALDEZ

(BORN 1998)

Kesz was born in the Philippines. When he was three, he lived as a scavenger, spending his days combing through a huge dumpsite in Cavite for scraps of metal or glass. He was forced to beg money for his father and survive on food he found among the litter. His family called him bad luck. They even tried to sell him.

At four, Kesz ran away from his parents, and lived sleeping in graveyards or doorways. One day he was pushed into a towering fire of rubbish, scorching one side of his body. It was both the most painful and the most hopeful day of his life; it was the day he met Harnin Manalaysay, the man who dressed his wounds and went on to become Kesz's guardian. It was the first time he'd been shown love.

Together with Harnin, Kesz formed Championing Community Children, C3 for short, an organization dedicated to educating street children in hygiene and providing them with packages, called Gifts of Hope, containing toys, toothbrushes, slippers and school supplies. The group expanded rapidly, attracting hundreds of volunteers and helping more and more children in the slums, dumps and shanty towns of Manila.

For his work with C3, Kesz won the Children's International Peace Prize, becoming the youngest person and first Filipino ever to win. The award came with $100,000 prize money. Kesz has donated it to causes he believes in and injected it into his own organization.

It has been twelve years since C3 was first established and they've helped over 38,000 street kids. Kesz himself has treated almost three thousand wounds.

To the street children of the Philippines, Kesz says, 'Do not lose hope.' To those more fortunate children with homes and families, he says, 'One is never too young to do something to help and meet a need.'

JESSICA COX

(BORN 1983)

Jessica had dreamed of flying from a young age. She would get frustrated with being different to everyone else, and found that imagining herself soaring through the sky above them all helped. What made her different? Jessica was born with a rare birth defect that means she has no arms.

She wore prosthetic arms because she felt she needed them to fit in. The arms were heavy and would get uncomfortable in the Arizona heat. At the age of fourteen, she made one of the biggest decisions of her life, and decided to stop wearing them. Instead she embraced her difference, learning how to handle everyday tasks with her feet. She hasn't looked back since.

Jessica drives, swims, dances, scuba dives, surfs, holds a degree in psychology, and has three black belts in taekwondo, which she won competing against people with both arms. She never felt disabled, she just knew she was differently abled.

She also learned to fly. As she was learning, new ways had to be found to enable her to do everything she needed to do in a plane, from buckling the seatbelt to starting the engine. Jessica didn't let it stop her. It took two instructors, with four planes, across three states, but she finally got her pilot's licence after three years of training. It had been a long journey.

In 2013 Jessica flew to Ethiopia. There, she met an eight-year-old boy called Tariku, who had also been born without arms. They ate together with their feet and Tariku introduced Jessica to injera, a kind of pancake bread popular in Africa. Seeing her fly herself out of his village on a plane, he must have felt there was nothing in the world he wasn't capable of.

Jessica's advice for people feeling isolated because of their disabilities?

'Develop self-confidence in your special abilities because there are things you can offer the world that other people can't.'

LIAM DAVIS

(BORN 1986)

Liam had fallen in with a bad crowd. He was ten but hanging out with older boys, getting arrested, and heading nowhere fast. That was when the manager of Grimsby Town told him if he could keep out of trouble, then they'd sign him to the youth team. Liam did, and his football career began.

When he got older, Liam fell in love with a man. He never kept his relationship a secret, but he never shouted about it either.

He kept playing football semi-professionally, training twice a week and working part-time in a café. When he joined a new club, Grimsborough, he went for a night out with the team and ended up mentioning his boyfriend. The rest of the boys were supportive. They told him that they had his back if he needed them.

One day, the national newspapers heard about Liam. 'Britain's Only Openly Gay Footballer', read the headlines. It was a shock to him and his team that the fact he was gay received so much attention; they'd always known and never cared.

Liam got some abuse on the pitch, but what's surprised him more than anything is the support he's received for being who he is. He'd like more footballers to feel safe enough to come out as gay. He understands how terrifying it could be walking out in front of thousands of people, not knowing how they're going to react to you, but he isn't sure why people in smaller teams like his are scared.

Currently, out of around five hundred players in the premier league, none are openly gay. Liam thinks it's likely that some of them are secretly gay but don't feel they would be accepted if they were to speak up.

What does he want? 'For someone else to think "I can do that. I'm brave and strong enough to do that".'

JOAN OF ARC

(1412-1431)

Joan grew up in the middle of The Hundred Years War, a long and bloody fight between the English and the French for the control of France. Her family owned a farm, where Joan worked tending animals and sewing clothes.

At thirteen, while playing in the garden, Joan claimed to have visions. She said she saw saints who urged her to rise up, drive the English out of France, and crown Charles VII king in a place called Reims.

Joan travelled with a family friend to a town called Vaucouleurs and presented herself to a garrison commander who was a supporter of Charles.

'I've been having visions,' she explained. 'And I think I should lead the French army.'

'Of course you do,' the commander said, laughing.

But the people of the town supported her. They put pressure on the commander until he had no choice but to send Joan, along with an armed escort, to see the king. To keep from attracting attention, she cut her hair off and wore men's clothes.

Charles was intrigued by the peasant girl who arrived at his court, asking to lead the French army into battle. No one knows why, but he gave her control of some men.

Spirits among the French forces were low. They often lost battles, even if they outnumbered the English armies fighting against them. This was exactly what was happening at Orleans, a French city that was under heavy attack from the English.

When Joan rode in, everything changed. The people cheered. They raised their swords and gladly charged when she ordered them to attack. The city was saved.

At Joan's insistence, Charles went to Reims and was crowned king.

A year later, Joan was captured. The English paid a huge amount of money for her because they knew how important she was to the French. They burned her at the stake. Some say her heart survived the fire.

On May 16th 1920, Joan was officially made a saint.

LUKE AMBLER

(BORN 1989)

One night, Luke Ambler was at his brother-in-law Andy's house, laughing, messing about, and playing games. A few days later, Andy took his own life.

It broke the hearts of everyone who knew him.

It was a shock but Luke knew how it felt to be down. He'd struggled with his own issues growing up, including an eating disorder and bullying. As a professional rugby player, he'd also felt the pressure of acting tough and manly, even while he'd been struggling with feeling sad or stressed.

He thinks that sometimes men and boys can feel too embarrassed or afraid to talk about their feelings and they end up bottling them up. Holding all those feelings in can get too much for a person. It can lead to them feeling as though they can't go on. That's what had happened to Andy.

Wanting to help other people who might be having similar trouble, Luke started the Andy's Man Club. The aim of the club is to provide a place for men to come and openly talk about their feelings, without fear of being judged or made fun of.

He also started a campaign on social media. He took a picture of himself doing an OK symbol and captioned it: It's Okay To Talk. Since then, celebrities from all walks of life have posted images of themselves in the same pose, trying to spread the word that there's no shame in speaking up about how you feel.

There's an old saying that goes 'a problem shared is a problem halved'. And there's even science to back it up! Experiments have shown that just talking about our problems can lead us to calm down and put things into perspective.

Luke's already had messages from people saying that he's saved them. Just remember, he says. It's okay to talk.

JUANA INÉS DE LA CRUZ

(1651-1695)

Juana Inés de la Cruz was born in 1651 in Mexico, which was not a time when girls were generally educated. But she first learned to read when she was three by following her sisters to their school and begging the teachers there to teach her.

'Mother,' Juana asked one day.
'Could I disguise myself as a boy and go to university?'

Her mother said no, but finally agreed to let Juana move away to study under a priest. She proved herself to be a prodigy. Juana learned Latin in twenty lessons and was soon writing poetry in four languages. She would hold discussions with philosophers, mathematicians, poets, and historians, all of whom would come away impressed.

News of Juana's intelligence spread across Mexico. She received several offers of marriage and refused every one. She was twenty when she joined the convent and became a nun purely to focus on studying.

There, Juana wrote and read on everything from history to love, and feminism to religion. She amassed a great library of over four thousand books and wrote several of her own.

But some powerful men were angry because of their belief that women shouldn't be allowed to pursue academic studies, and that God wouldn't approve.

It frustrated Juana greatly.

'Who has forbidden women to engage in private and individual studies?' she wrote. 'Have they not a rational soul as men do?'

Eventually, she sold all of her books and gave the money to the poor. While caring for nuns who were sick with the plague, Juana caught it too, and she died. Her old convent has since become a university named after her. Juana is remembered today in paintings, plays, and films all over the world.

MOHAMED TAHER

A recent report by the United Nations found that 99.3% of Egyptian women said they were being harassed simply for walking down the street. They were touched, shouted at, and made to feel unsafe. Given the conditions, many women preferred to stay at home.

Inspired by the project of a photographer called Dane Shitagi in which professional ballerinas were photographed on the streets of New York, Mohamed wondered whether a similar idea could help the women of Cairo to reclaim the streets of their city.

He got in contact with all the dancers he could find. 'We got a lot of comments from girls saying they want to do this,' he said. 'They want to dance on the street. They want to feel free.'

With his camera and various dancers, Mohamed headed out onto the streets of Cairo. They left early in the mornings, for the clearest light and to avoid the crowds, and Mohamed captured images of the women expressing themselves openly and without fear. The grace and beauty of ballet placed against the hectic roughness of bustling city streets made for a beautiful series of photographs and a powerful message of no longer living in fear.

Although some women were initially hesitant about taking part, afraid of the reactions they'd get from people walking past, the responses were almost all positive. Most people were surprised but excited to find ballerinas in the streets of their traditionally conservative country. They would stop the ballerinas politely and ask for photos, posing alongside them.

Egyptian authorities have now increased the punishment for sexual harassment. But changing laws doesn't necessarily mean changing minds. Mohamed hopes that projects such as his will help change further how the women of Egypt are viewed and treated.

JULIETTE GORDON LOW

(1860-1927)

Juliette Gordon Low was born in Savannah, Georgia. Her parents called her Daisy. Her siblings called her Crazy Daisy. They never quite knew what she'd do next.

Since childhood, Daisy had struggled with hearing problems from an ear infection. On her wedding day, a piece of rice was thrown into her ear, and the hearing in it disappeared altogether. It was the start of an unhappy marriage. Her husband died when she was forty-five, when they were living in Great Britain, and Daisy had no idea what to do with herself next. She decided to travel the world, seeing the tallest pyramids of Egypt and the deepest jungles of India before returning to England.

There, Daisy met a man called Robert Baden-Powell. Robert was the founder of the Boy Scouts and through him Daisy became involved with the Girl Guides. She started her own patrol in Scotland and taught the girls how to camp, read maps, tie knots, and light fires.

It amazed her how profound the effects of being out in nature could be. By teaching the girls how to be self-sustaining, Daisy could give them a confidence they'd never before found in themselves.

There were other girl groups at the time, but they thought the things Daisy was teaching were not suitable for young ladies. Girls should be learning to sew and clean, they said. Not messing around in the dirt.

Daisy knew that made no sense. She wanted to bring practical skills, confidence, and the freedom of the outdoors to as many girls as possible. So she set sail back to America and telephoned her cousin, saying: 'I've got something for the girls of Savannah, and all of America, and all the world, and we're going to start it tonight!'

Millions of girls and hundreds of patrols would soon be spread across the whole of the United States.

In 1927, Daisy died. Her candlelit funeral was attended by hundreds of Girl Guides. By 2017, over fifty million girls had grown up as members of the organization, including Taylor Swift, Michelle Obama and Mariah Carey.

NAOTO MATSUMURA

(BORN 1960)

In March 2011, a severe earthquake rocked Japan, causing huge tsunami waves to flood the land. When they hit the Fukushima power plant, its reactors exploded, and radiation spread around the surrounding area. Everyone who lived within thirty kilometres was evacuated. Exposure to the radiation could cause sickness, hair loss, cancer, and even death.

As people fled Fukushima, they left behind all kinds of animals tied up in barns, trapped in coops, and locked in houses. Naoto returned a few months after the disaster to find them either dying or dead from lack of food.

The government wanted all the surviving animals killed, though they'd been exposed to such high levels of radiation that they wouldn't be eaten. Naoto wouldn't let that happen. He decided that if no one else was going to do it, he'd have to move back and look after them all. It was thanks to him that the government agreed not to kill the remaining animals.

Now Naoto lives alone, with only the animals for company. There are fifty cows, two ostriches, over a hundred cats, dogs, and various other pets and livestock who are reliant on him.

Naoto knows that living inside the evacuated zone is dangerous. He doesn't care. He couldn't just let the animals to fend for themselves. When his grown-up children called from Tokyo, Naoto told them, 'Don't worry, if the whole world dies from this nuclear disaster, I'm still not going to die. I'm not going to leave here.'

KATIE SANDWINA

(1884-1952)

Katie was the second oldest of fifteen children. Her parents were circus performers who travelled across Europe astounding audiences with their unbelievable feats of strength. At the age of two, Katie could handstand on her father's hands. It was obvious she had a natural talent for the family business.

She trained in gymnastics and started lifting weights when she became a teenager. When the family visited towns to perform, Katie's father would offer any men in the audience one hundred German marks if they could wrestle her and win. The reward would have been over a thousand pounds in today's money. Still, no one ever beat her.

One of the most famous strongmen of the time was a man called Eugen Sandow. Many people at the time believed he was the most perfectly formed human in the world.

After one performance in New York, Katie asked the crowd whether anyone wanted to face her in a weightlifting competition.

Eugen was in the crowd. He raised his hand. As he stepped up to the stage, the audience clearly thought there was no way Katie had a chance.

Each of them took it in turns to lift a weight up and over their heads with one hand. Steadily, they increased the size of the dumbbells. At three hundred pounds, about the same weight as a fully-grown panda, Katie easily cleared hers. Eugen could barely lift his to his chest. The crowd were amazed and Katie was propelled to fame.

Eventually, she settled down and opened a restaurant with her husband. Sometimes, when the mood took her, she'd stun customers by bending steel or casually lifting her husband up over her head.

It was fun to remind them that you never know what to expect from a person. Which is exactly what Katie had done all her life.

OCEAN VUONG

(BORN 1988)

During the Vietnam War, an American soldier fell in love with a Vietnamese woman who worked in the rice paddies. Together, they had three children. One of these children was Ocean's mother.

Eventually the American soldier returned to the US to visit his family. While he was gone, the city of Saigon fell, US troops evacuated, and life became tumultuous for thousands of people. Ocean's mother and her siblings were separated and put into orphanages. Ocean was born on a rice farm.

After time in a refugee camp, seven members of the family made it to America with Ocean, where they lived together in a one-room apartment. None of them could read in any language. In the evenings, they would gather round his grandmother to hear stories that transported them back home.

Ocean studied as hard as he could, wanting to make his family proud. It was hard. He was picked on and his dyslexia meant he was slower with words than the other kids.

He made it to university, but struggled so much that he dropped out after eight weeks. Afraid of telling his mother, he slept on friends' sofas. That was when Ocean discovered the thrill of the New York poetry scene and started writing himself.

Without high hopes, Ocean put together a collection of his poems and sent it off to a competition. *Night Sky With Exit Wounds* went on to win not just that competition, but various prizes in America and England.

The cover of his book was a photograph of Ocean, at two years old, in a refugee camp with his mother and aunt. That photo cost them three tins of rice at the time. Since his success, Ocean has been able to buy his mum a house with a garden.

Ocean knows that without the war, he would never have been born. It's a hard thing to think about, but sometimes life is complicated that way.

KENOJUAK ASHEVAK

(1927-2013)

Kenojuak was born in an igloo on the coast of Baffin Island, inside the Arctic circle. Her father was a hunter and a shaman who could predict the weather and call fish to the surface of the water so they could be caught. Growing up, Kenojuak learned traditional Inuit crafts, like how to sew together the skins of seals and make waterproof clothes with reindeer sinew.

One day, when nurses visited her village, they found that Kenojuak was suffering from tuberculosis and she was sent to Quebec City to recover. She had to leave behind her husband, her seven birth children, and her seven adopted children.

It was then that Kenojuak discovered art.

For three years she remained in hospital, and she spent those years doll-making, drawing, and sculpting, despite her illness. When she was finally allowed home, Kenojuak carried on creating art alongside her husband. Her colourful, bizarre depictions of Arctic animals and native people were quickly recognized outside of her small community for their beauty and uniqueness. Her designs became some of the first ever done by an Inuk woman to be made into prints.

In 1963, a documentary called *Eskimo Artist* was made about Kenojuak. The money from it meant that her husband could buy his own canoe and hunt on his own to provide food for their family. Soon her work was appearing in shows around the world, receiving awards and selling in galleries. One of her pieces, *Enchanted Owl*, was put on Canadian stamps, and another was put on the ten dollar note.

With the money from her art, Kenojuak could help her family, buying supplies for her kids and dance and swimming lessons for her grandkids. She says helping each other is the Inuit way. But money was never the point. What was her main goal? According to Kenojuak, 'to make something beautiful, that's all'.

ORVILLE WRIGHT

(1871-1948)

& WILBUR WRIGHT

(1867-1912)

The Wright brothers were born four years apart, with Wilbur being the eldest. Their father, a bishop, travelled a lot and often brought the boys back gifts. One day he returned with a model helicopter powered by an elastic band. The brothers immediately set about building replicas of it.

One day Wilbur lost his teeth while playing hockey. The injury made him shy, and he stopped going to school. Their mother had fallen sick so he stayed at home, caring for her and reading books from his father's library. When their mother died, Orville dropped out of school too.

Bicycling had swept the nation, and the Wrights went into business mending twisted wheels and punctured tyres. The brothers were soon capable of building their own bikes. Wright Cycle Company was born and business boomed. But they had other ambitions.

Newspapers were filled with stories of people trying, and failing, to build and fly aircraft. The problem wasn't getting airborne, but controlling them once they were up. The Wright brothers focused on trying to build a working control system.

They headed to Kitty Hawk, North Carolina, to start tests. First, they added their control system to a glider. Then began the long, hard task of constructing a suitable engine. Years later, after countless crashes, the brothers had built the first practical, controllable aeroplane, the Wright 1905, without any formal training or education.

Wilbur died in 1912. Orville was deeply saddened by the destruction planes were made to carry out in subsequent wars. But he could be proud, too, of the unprecedented way in which they've gone on to connect people.

KIM SOO-NYUNG

(BORN 1971)

When she was nine, one of Kim's teachers recommended she try archery because she was taller than the other kids and her arms were long. She started shooting straight away.

Years of dedication saw Kim compete at the 1988 Seoul Olympics in Korea, where she was born. She was just seventeen years old. On the last round of the final, she shot nine arrows from thirty metres and every single one hit the bullseye. Kim walked away from that Olympics with two gold medals and the deafening sound of her home country's applause ringing in her ears.

People started calling her The Viper because she was so powerful and precise. For a period of time, Kim held every single outdoor archery record there was.

At the next Olympics, she left with one gold and one silver. That was when Kim put down her bow to raise a family. She married, had two children, and lived a life away from the archery range. But she wasn't quite done.

Six years after last holding a bow, Kim decided she wasn't ready to give up the sport altogether. She trained as hard as she could for eight months and qualified for the 2000 Sydney Olympics. It was tougher than it had been before and Kim was up against younger opponents who'd been training for far longer than she had. She left the games with one bronze and one gold medal, making her the most decorated Korean athlete of all time.

In 2011, the archery federation declared Kim the best female archer of the twentieth century.

She has since turned to coaching, doing everything she can to push the sport forward. In 2012, Kim travelled to the US to learn about new techniques and bows so that she could better train her own team. That year, the Korean women thrashed their opponents and took home gold.

Kim proved to the world that it's never too late to get to where you want to be.

PETER JACKSON

(BORN 1961)

Peter Jackson was born on Halloween. Growing up an only child in Pukerua Bay, a small seaside town in New Zealand, he had to make his own fun. At first, this meant watching old monster films like *Godzilla* and *King Kong*. By the time he was nine, it meant trying to make his own movies.

With his parents' camera and his friends acting out the parts he gave them, Peter made a World War Two film. He dug holes in the garden for trenches. To give the effect of gunfire, he cut holes in the film so it flashed as it played.

To try and fund his first full film, Peter got a job at a newspaper called *The Evening Post*. Using only his own money, he spent four years making a film about aliens who come to earth to capture humans and use them as ingredients for their intergalactic fast food chain. Filmed at weekends, all the parts were again played by friends and neighbours. Peter built the models himself and created all the special effects. The film was called *Bad Taste*. It was bizarre, disgusting, funny, and unlike anything else that was being made.

Amazingly, the film was shown at the biggest film festival in the world: Cannes. Some people found it revolting, some loved it. It went on to be played in thirty countries around the world. Peter was twenty-six and he quit his job at the newspaper, ready to devote himself full-time to film.

After making a series of horror films, Peter was offered the chance to direct an adaptation of one of his favourite books: *The Lord of the Rings*. It became one of the most successful film franchises of all time, as people around the world followed the adventures of a plucky hobbit called Frodo, his escort of dwarves and elves, and their quest to destroy the one ring.

After finishing *Lord of the Rings*, Peter finally got to make his own version of *King Kong*. 'I truly believe this is the best version of *Kong* ever released,' wrote one reviewer. The film won three Oscars. Peter had come a long way from the films he'd made in his parents' garden with his friends.

LADY GODIVA

(990 AD-1067)

In Medieval England, the people of Coventry were suffering under heavy taxes. Their lord, Leofric, was forcing everyone to pay money towards growing the king's army. As a result, they were poor and unhappy.

But Leofric's wife, Godiva, cared for the people. She couldn't bear that they survived miserably on bread and water, while she and her husband had everything they wanted. She pleaded with her husband to lower the taxes. She'd seen what had happened in Worcester when taxes had been too high: the people had murdered the tax collector and in retaliation the king had ordered their entire town destroyed.

'Please,' she asked again. 'Lower the taxes.'

'Never,' he told her. 'You'd have to ride naked through the streets on a horse before I'd even consider it.'

And that's exactly what she did. On a snow-white horse, with only her long veils of golden hair to cover her body, Godiva galloped through the centre of Coventry.

Out of respect for her, all of the towns-people remained inside with their windows and doors shut. When one man opened his window to sneak a look at Lady Godiva, he was struck blind.

Leofric was amazed. True to his word, he repealed the heavy taxes and had a religious experience, which led to the founding of a monastery.

Godiva's generosity didn't stop there. After her husband died, she used the money she inherited to give gifts to various religious institutions, including the arm of St Augustine, a priceless relic that had come from Rome.

She has not been forgotten. Countless pieces of art, songs and films have been made about Lady Godiva's selfless journey through the streets of her town.

In the centre of Coventry, looking down over the market square, is the Godiva clock. Every hour, on the hour, the clock chimes, a door slides open, and a mechanical Lady Godiva trots out, naked on the back of a snow-white horse.

POPE FRANCIS

(BORN 1936)

Ever since the time of Jesus, there has been a pope. Whenever one pope steps down or dies, 120 cardinals barricade themselves inside The Sistine Chapel, sealing the doors until they've decided who will take his place. The world waits with bated breath for white smoke to emerge from the chimney, signalling a decision has been made.

On March 13th 2013, Francis became the 266th pope, the head of the Catholic church around the world.

He was the first pope to come from Latin America and the first to choose the name Francis. But those weren't the only ways he was different.

Francis didn't live in the fancy penthouse of all the other popes, but took a tiny room in a guesthouse. He made it clear he wouldn't be going to the grand summer residence available to all popes. Instead, he wanted to help his people.

He kissed the feet of prisoners, agreed to selfies, donated money, and met tribes in the Amazon who were having their homes destroyed by loggers. Francis sold his Harley Davidson motorcycle to fund a hostel for the poor. He fired a bishop who spent too much money on a big house and turned the house into a soup kitchen for those who couldn't afford to eat.

As leader of the Catholic church, the pope tends to hold very traditional values and beliefs. Not Francis. When asked about his feelings on gay people, Pope Francis replied, 'Who am I to judge?' It may not sound like much, but the Catholic church has traditionally spoken out against being gay, so it marked a big step forward.

Many members of the Catholic church were appalled.

Francis didn't care. He stood up and spoke out against them, giving a rousing speech in which he condemned those acting with closed hearts. He doesn't think the Bible should be used as a tool to judge people. To Francis, it's an inspiration to show love to whoever needs it.

LETICIA BUFONI

(BORN 1993)

At nine years old, Leticia was skateboarding in the graffiti-scrawled parks of São Paulo, Brazil. The only other people riding alongside her were boys. Leticia's dad didn't approve.

'Skateboarding is for boys,' he told her. 'You're not skating any more.' And to prove it, he broke her skateboard in half.

Leticia didn't even think about listening. She built another board and went straight back out to ride the ramps the next day. Seeing her come back home, blood streaming from her knees, her father shook his head. It didn't look like there was anything he could do to stop her.

So he travelled with Leticia to California to compete in the X Games, the biggest event in the world for extreme sports. Watching her practise the same trick over and over, trying to perfect it, he could see how dedicated she was. He told her that if she got the trick right on her next try, she could stay in America to skate.

She got it, and so she stayed.

Every day, Leticia worked as hard as she could, mastering more and more difficult tricks on higher and higher ramps. She was sponsored by Nike and Red Bull and lots of other sports companies who were so impressed they wanted to help on her journey. Aerials, grabs, grinds, and flips; Leticia wanted to master them all.

When she was twenty, Leticia became the first ever female athlete to win three gold medals in one X Games.

Back in Brazil, she's recognized everywhere she goes and has even been given her own TV show. More than anything, Leticia's thrilled that more girls will be inspired to pick up a skateboard.

Skateboarding's being added to the Olympics in 2020. Leticia wants to bring home a gold medal to the father who once told her she could never skate again.

ROBERT SMITH

(BORN 1959)

Robert's guitar teacher thought he was terrible, so he quit lessons and learned by ear instead, painstakingly working out how to play the songs he heard coming from the radio. He bought his own guitar after saving up twenty pounds.

Robert also started wearing make-up as a teenager. He liked the reactions it got. People would scream at him, which he found both strange and hilarious. He once wore a dress to school. None of the teachers said anything, but some boys beat him up at the end of the day. He didn't find that so funny, but he wouldn't stop being himself.

It was at school that he formed a band called The Cure with four of his friends. They played their first show together in front of their classmates when they were thirteen. The band was searching for a singer but couldn't find one, so Robert agreed to do it, even though he hated the sound of his voice.

He wore smeared red lipstick, black make-up around his eyes, and hairsprayed his hair into a giant bird's nest.

The Cure wrote songs for when you wanted to bounce around the room smiling, and they wrote songs for when you wanted to be alone, hiding under a blanket. They wrote songs for kids who felt like they didn't fit in. People called them goths, punks, new wave rockers. But Robert and his friends didn't call themselves anything but The Cure.

When they went to record their first big album, the producer was shocked by Robert's twenty-pound guitar.

'What's that?' he asked. 'You can't play with that.'

So Robert went out and bought a new one, but secretly had parts of his old one built into it.

'I'm not technically a good player,' he said, 'but at least I don't sound like anyone else.'

In 1989, The Cure played to 44,000 people in the New York Giants' stadium. The band went on to sell over twenty-seven million records. Robert still wears lipstick, still hairsprays his hair, and still plays with the parts of his first guitar.

LISE MEITNER

(1878-1968)

In 1944, a German chemist called Otto Hahn received the Nobel Prize in Chemistry, one of the most prestigious awards you can receive. His lab partner of thirty years, Lise Meitner, was completely overlooked, even though they had worked together.

Lise was born in Vienna, in 1878, the third child of eight. Austrian laws meant women weren't allowed to go to college but her father paid for her to have a private education and she went on to become the second woman ever to graduate from the University of Vienna with a degree.

Lise focused her studies on physics – radioactivity, specifically. She worked together with Otto to isolate various isotopes and observe them as they decayed.

In 1923, Lise discovered something called radiationless transition. Just as she would be years later, she was overlooked. The effect was named after a French man who discovered it a full two years after she did.

When the Nazis took control of Austria, Lise fled. Her family were Jewish and they risked being sent to concentration camps and killed. Otto stayed.

In Copenhagen, Lise worked alongside her nephew to explain a process she had discovered with Otto called nuclear fission. Nuclear fission involves splitting a large atom into smaller atoms. When it occurs, unbelievable amounts of energy are released. For that reason, nuclear weapons had devastating potential, while nuclear power had the potential to provide huge quantities of electricity. Today, around eleven per cent of the world's power comes from fission happening inside nuclear reactors.

Finally, in 1992, Lise got some recognition. When the extremely reactive element number 109 was discovered, it was named in her honour. They called it meitnerium.

ROBERTA COWELL

(1918-2011)

Robert Cowell had been obsessed with fast cars and big planes ever since he was a child. He joined the RAF as soon as he was old enough to do so. Unfortunately, he got sick in the air and had to drop out, so he turned to motor racing and sped along the ground instead.

When the Second World War broke out, Robert decided to rejoin the RAF and successfully flew Tiger Moths and Spitfires in air battles with the Nazis. During one mission, he was blinded by thick cloud and almost crashed into the sea, just managing to land on a cliff before his petrol had run out.

Another time, he blacked out while flying, barely coming around in time to regain control. When he went down over Germany, Robert was taken captive and held for five months in a prisoner-of-war camp. He taught the other prisoners about cars and their engines. Sometimes they'd get so hungry they'd have to kill and eat the camp cats.

Once the war was over, Robert was sent home to England and focused his energies on motor racing.

But he never felt comfortable, never felt quite right. After seeing different psychologists, Robert started to realize that this was because he'd been born in the wrong body. Though he had the physical features of a male, he knew inside he was female, and he wanted a body to match.

So he began the long and difficult process of changing his body from a male body to a female one. The surgery was illegal, and to have it done, Robert had to leave behind his family, and tell the world that he had always had a female body. Robert became Roberta. She became the first person in Britain to go through the process.

Her change meant that Roberta couldn't race the Grand Prix any more, though she never stopped being involved in racing and never stopped flying planes.

Through the war, through the loneliness, and through her battle to become her true self, Roberta never once slowed down.

LOUJAIN AL-HATHLOUL

(BORN 1989)

For a long time, women in Saudi Arabia have struggled to gain the rights given to the men. They weren't allowed to vote until 2015, compete in the Olympics until 2012, and still aren't allowed to open their own bank accounts.

Up until 2017, women were also forbidden from driving. Loujain set out to change that.

She had grown up in a conservative area of Saudi Arabia but moved away to France as a teenager. While an adult in Canada, she started making videos on an app called Keek, which would allow thirty-second recordings. She posted videos of herself with her face uncovered and her hair flowing free as she drove a car, all of which were illegal for women in Saudi Arabia. Loujain believed that the ability to drive could be the symbol that would give women there more independence and lead to further freedoms being unlocked.

Some people criticized her for posting from the safety of a country where the Saudi authorities couldn't reach her. So Loujain flew home. Her father met her at the airport and gave her the keys to his car and she drove, filming the whole thing. The authorities called her father in and made him swear never to let his daughter drive again. Loujain didn't give up.

A few days after her wedding, she drove from Abu Dhabi across the desert to Saudi Arabia and demanded to be let across the border. This time she was arrested and put in jail for seventy-three days. To be released, Loujain had to sign a document saying she wouldn't make any more videos discussing women's rights in Saudi Arabia. She signed it, happily, because the document didn't say anything about speaking out in writing. And she carried on doing just that.

On May 15th 2018, Loujain was once again arrested at her house because of her fight for equality. But thanks to the awareness she's raised about the plight of her country's women, the eyes of the world are on the Saudi Arabia government, and they are being urged by organizations everywhere to release peaceful protestors and grant women the rights they deserve.

HH
Hamilton Heights
High School

RYAN WHITE

(1971-1990)

AIDS is a syndrome caused by the HIV virus. It leads the body to grow weaker and less able to stand up to disease. Although it's more manageable with medicines we have today, forty years ago the disease meant that sufferers rarely lived for long after contracting it.

Ryan White was a schoolboy who caught the disease after being treated with blood infected with the HIV virus. Doctors gave him six months to live.

Despite his illness, Ryan tried to return to school. Parents and teachers made sure he wasn't allowed. Many people at the time didn't understand that HIV can only be transmitted through blood. They thought that Ryan would be a danger to the other children and they didn't want him anywhere near them.

On the one day Ryan was allowed back into school, more than half of the other children didn't turn up. The people Ryan delivered newspapers to started cancelling their subscriptions.

It broke Ryan's heart because he knew he wasn't a threat, and he set about trying to educate the public about AIDS and raise money for those suffering from it. Although he wouldn't live to see it, Ryan's efforts would play a great role in developing treatments for AIDS and making those treatments available.

After the bullying, Ryan's family moved to a different town and he joined a different high school. The people there had been educated about AIDS. Students at school shook Ryan's hand without being afraid and he was welcomed.

Ryan lived five years longer than the doctors had expected him to. He died on April 8th 1990. Over fifteen hundred people attended his funeral. On the day of the funeral, President Reagan wrote a tribute to Ryan in *The Washington Post*. 'We owe it to Ryan to be compassionate, caring, and tolerant toward those with AIDS,' he wrote. 'It's the disease that's frightening, not the people who have it.'

LYDA CONLEY

(1869-1946)

In the 1640s, the people of the Wyandot Nation were driven out of their homeland by white settlers. They were forced to live in Ohio, then moved again in the 1840s to Kansas, where they created a cemetery for their people. Seventy years later, that cemetery was sold to the government so that they could develop the land.

Lyda didn't think it was right.

'Why should we not be proud of our ancestors and protect their graves?' she asked. Her grandmother, mother, sister, aunts, and uncles were buried there, and she wasn't going to allow houses to be built over their bodies.

So she marched to the cemetery, built a shack inside it, and stayed there as a guard, armed with a shotgun. She and her sisters put up 'No Trespassing' signs and took shifts keeping watch with their guns.

In 1907, Lyda went and argued her case before the Supreme Court, becoming the first female Native American lawyer to do so. They rejected her appeal. Still, she refused to move from the cemetery.

In 1912, a police officer entered the graveyard and Lyda shot him. In her opinion, she had every right to protect the land of her people. She was arrested and put in jail.

But Lyda was drawing more and more attention and support from across the state. By 1916, a bill was passed that protected the land from being sold or developed.

Even though her battle had been won, Lyda continued spending her days in the cemetery, wandering among the graves and caring for the birds and squirrels.

When Lyda died, she was buried with her ancestors, in the cemetery she had spent her whole life protecting. In 2016, it was named a National Historic Landmark.

SAROO BRIERLEY

(BORN 1981)

From the age of five, Saroo Brierley would beg for food with his two older brothers, Guddu and Kallu. Sometimes Guddu would earn extra money by sweeping train carriages at night in their local station of Ganesh Talai, India. One evening, Saroo went with him. He got tired and lay down to sleep on the platform. Guddu promised to come back for him later.

When Saroo woke up, his brother was nowhere to be seen. He paced up and down the dark platform, calling his brother's name.

No answer. Thinking he might be on a train, Saroo climbed aboard the next one and fell asleep. When he woke, he couldn't get the door open. Lush hills, green fields, and hectic towns flashed past. Eventually, someone at the final station let him out. Saroo didn't know it yet, but he was nearly a thousand miles from home.

He lived homeless on the streets for months before being taken to a centre for abandoned children. They tried to trace his family but Saroo didn't know the name of his hometown.

Eventually he was adopted by an Australian family and grew up by the bright blue water and golden sands of Tasmania. He learned English and forgot Hindi. But he didn't forget his family.

As an adult, Saroo started using huge maps from Google Earth to try and track down his family. He followed all of the railway lines from the station he was found at, wracking his brain to try and remember anything about where he'd come from. Finally, something jogged his memory: a fountain beside the train tracks where he used to play.

In 2012, Saroo travelled to Khandwa. He met his mother, his sister, and one of his brothers. That's when he learned the tragic news that his brother Guddu had been hit by a train and died on the night they got separated.

Saroo now speaks regularly with his family in India and has bought his mother a house. A Hollywood film was made about his life. Saroo wants any other lost children to know that they should never give up on one day finding their home.

MARGARETE STEIFF

(1847-1909)

Margarete was a perfectly healthy child for the first eighteen months of her life. Then, tragedy struck. She came down with an illness that paralyzed her legs and left her almost entirely unable to move her right arm.

Despite her illness, Margarete started school early, never missed a day, and excelled in her lessons. Every day her siblings would wheel her to the schoolhouse in a cart and a neighbour would carry her up the stairs to the classroom.

One day, Margarete told her family she was going to become a seamstress. Everyone thought she'd fail but Margarete paid them no attention. By seventeen, she was using a sewing machine and had a small business making clothes out of felt.

At Christmas, Margarete used some of the felt to make elephants that were given out to children. They were cherished by everyone who received one.

Most toys at the time were made out of hard things that couldn't be cuddled and Margarete's soft animals were a much more comforting alternative. Margarete could see that kids wanted her creations so she continued making them even after the first elephants were gone. On the back of her clothing catalogue, she wrote: 'Children's toys in felt, safe and unbreakable. Elephants with colourful saddles.' Steiff toys was born.

Margarete's brother, Fritz, encouraged her to grow the business. He arranged for a new building to house the business, including an apartment with easy disabled access where Margarete could live comfortably and independently. She began making pigs, dogs, mice, cats, monkeys, and donkeys, all out of cuddly felt.

Then her brother hit on the idea of creating a bear. Steiff made some of the very first teddy bears in existence. You could tell they were genuine Steiffs by the button tags sewn into their ears.

By 1907, almost a million were being made every year. Steiff toys remain some of the most collectible, desirable, and loved toys around today. Their company motto is still: 'Only the best is good enough for our children!'

SAVION GLOVER

(BORN 1973)

Savion always had a feel for the beat. From the age of three, he was drumming on everything in sight. When his talent was noticed, he was invited to join a band, playing alongside a bassist, a saxophonist, and a pianist.

One day the band had a gig at the Broadway Dance Center. That was where Savion first witnessed rhythm tap, performed by dancers called hoofers. Different from the more showy musical style, this type of dancing had been created by slaves forbidden from playing their drums, which was what they had done culturally as a way of communicating with each other. By using their feet instead, they had created a means of expression that was private to them, and would not be understood by the slave-owners. As an African-American, Savion wanted to continue expressing the history of his people through dance.

He followed the beat into tap dancing and was soon cast in a production of *The Tap Dance Kid*. In the musical, Savion played a boy named Willie who dreamed of one day making it as a dancer. Willie's father was a serious lawyer, who fought against his son's ambitions, but is eventually won round by his son's determination and talent.

Savion calls his style of tap 'hitting'. It's heavy, loud, and relentless. Instead of traditional patterns and moves, it makes room for wild bursts of emotion and improvisation. And it isn't just the style, but the set-ups that Savion has experimented with. In one piece, three dancers performed completely alone, unaccompanied by any music, with microphones in their shoes. In another, Savion wore a tuxedo and pounded across the stage as a full orchestra played sweeping arrangements of classical music around him.

In 2006, Savion brought the world joy through tap when he put together dances for the animated film *Happy Feet*, about a penguin who couldn't sing like the other penguins, and had to speak through his feet instead.

Savion still sees the dance as a means of reminding others what Africans went through. People have called him 'the man who saved tap'.

MARIA LORENA BARROS

(1948-1976)

In the 1960s, students across the Philippines were protesting against the government. They protested against the price of education, the rights of workers, and the police attacking those who stood up for their beliefs. These were dark times and the president ruled with terror.

Maria was raised by her mother. She was curious about a lot of things, especially why some people were very rich and so many others were very poor.

As she didn't have siblings, Maria read books to stop herself getting lonely. She fell in love with theatre, gymnastics, and writing. At university she focused on anthropology, the study of how humans behave. During the student protests, she marched for her belief that everyone had a right to be equal.

When the police advanced on her university in 1970, aiming guns at the building, Maria barricaded herself inside with the other students.

After that, Maria decided she had to take action. She thought that a women's organization was needed in the Philippines. She started one and the group grew and grew, picking up members in villages, factories, and schools.

A year later, new rules meant the police could arrest whoever they wanted, whenever they wanted. Maria was charged, arrested, and sent to a prison camp. She made her escape twelve months later.

She lived in hiding, writing poems, songs, and essays that criticized the government and inspired those who fought against them. One day she was caught and injured in a shootout. Her captors said they could save her if she would give them information about her group. She refused to say anything. Even the threat of death wasn't enough to get her to give up on her beliefs.

At only twenty-eight years old, Maria was given a heroine's funeral, where revolutionary songs were sung and stories were told of her courage and strength. Maria continues to be an inspiration to Filipinos, a symbol of darker times and the light that they can bring out in us.

MAKIBAKA

SHAH RUKH KHAN

(BORN 1965)

During long evenings in New Delhi, Shah Rukh Khan's family would gather round the radio to hear songs from Hindi films. As the songs played, Shah Rukh Khan would dance and sing among his relatives. When the music stopped, he'd venture outside to play cricket under the streetlights.

At school, everyone was amazed by Shah Rukh Khan's impersonations of the great Bollywood actors. Bollywood is the name used for Indian cinema, and its films are even bigger than Hollywood's, with over a billion more tickets sold every year. The films tend to be long, colourful, and packed with singing and dancing.

His passion meant that Shah Rukh Khan spent more time in the theatre than at school. When his father died, performing was where he found comfort, but his sister fell into a depression and it was up to Shah Rukh Khan to take care of her.

When his mother fell ill, Shah Rukh Khan decided he had to make it as an actor to help his family. He moved to Mumbai, where the Bollywood industry is based, with no money and nowhere to stay. He slept on roads and was thrown out of houses when he couldn't pay rent.

But once Shah Rukh Khan got his break, he captured the hearts of people throughout India and beyond. He became one of the biggest actors in the world, and the richest.

The money he makes doesn't go to waste: Shah Rukh Khan does great charity work, though most of it is kept private, because he doesn't think you should do charity just for the attention.

Shah Rukh Khan lives with his wife, his children, and the sister he's still taking care of. He's even bought his own cricket team. But he doesn't take everything for granted. 'Success and failure are both part of life,' he says. 'Both are not permanent.'

MARIA SPELTERINI

(1853-1912)

Niagara Falls is the name given to three thundering waterfalls that sit on the border between Canada and America. The falls are over 12,000 years old, over a mile wide, and drop over seventy Olympic swimming pools' worth of water every minute.

They are devastatingly beautiful and extremely dangerous. Even now, they continue to claim lives, year after year, as people fall in by accident.

But Maria wasn't afraid.

Born in Italy, Maria was raised in a circus troupe and began performing at the age of three. When she grew up, she toured alone across Europe, before crossing the Atlantic Ocean to America.

At the age of only twenty-three, Maria performed a daring feat to celebrate the 100th anniversary of America gaining independence from Great Britain. On a wire that was only 5.7 centimetres thick, she crossed the almost hundred-metre-long Niagara Gorge as the waters raged below her. Audiences were stunned. Maria thought it was easy.

So she made another attempt, a few days later. This time she wore huge woven baskets on her feet.

Still, too easy.

A week later, she crossed again. This time completely blindfolded.

And she made it.

In her final crossing, Maria walked with her arms and legs chained together. She still managed the entire tightrope walk without faltering.

Maria wasn't always so lucky. On May 5th 1877, she was crossing a tightrope on a bicycle when it broke and she fell from a great height. The audience was shocked and terrified.

Maria survived, proof of the astonishing and amazingly dangerous things human beings are capable of.

SIMÓN BOLÍVAR

(1783-1830)

From 1492, Spanish explorers called *Conquistadors* began sailing across the Atlantic Ocean and seizing control of parts of America. They enslaved native people, killed others, spread disease, and carried away huge amounts of gold and silver to pay for their wars in Europe.

Simón first learned all of this in 1799, when he moved to Spain after his parents died. He had grown up in Venezuela in South America, in a rich family whose money came from gold and copper mines. While he was in Europe, Simón studied history, philosophy, and literature. He went on rambling walks with one of his old teachers, where they discussed ideas about what it means to be free.

Returning to his homeland, Simón declared that he wanted to start a revolution. He wanted to lead the people of South America as they fought for their freedom after three hundred years of rule by the Spanish.

He gathered a group of soldiers who shared his dream, armed them, and marched alongside them over hundreds of miles of jungle, swamp, and dry plains. Deep in the Andes mountains, Simón's group of revolutionaries fought the royalists and won. It was the start of a long and complicated period of battles, time spent in hiding, and assassination attempts.

In 1819, Simón was made president of the first union of South American countries and the country of Bolivia was named in his honour. Five years later, on December 9th, the Battle of Ayacucho took place and the Spanish forces were defeated once and for all.

People called Simón 'The Liberator' because he was determined to set them free.

Ultimately, Simón didn't just liberate Venezuela. He also helped Bolivia, Panama, Colombia, Ecuador, and Peru to free themselves from Spanish rule too. Today, his birthday is a national holiday.

MEGAN HINE

(BORN 1984)

If you were ever stuck on a tropical island, lost in a jungle, or stranded in a desert, Megan is the person you would want by your side. She knows which bugs to eat, how to start a fire, and the best way to filter your own pee if you ever need to drink it.

Megan always felt trapped as a child. She yearned to be outside in nature, having adventures, rather than stuck in a grey classroom staring at textbooks. Playing tennis at school, she'd hit the ball as hard as she could out of the court, so that she could spend the rest of the lesson hunting through the wild undergrowth for it.

Megan joined the military cadets when she was a teenager as a way of spending more time outdoors. It saw her white-water kayaking, ice climbing, and heading off on long treks through the country.

She's since taught off-road driving in the Lake District and rafting in the Alps. Now Megan spends most of the year on her own in the wilderness. With just a backpack, some medicine and an axe, she cuts her own path through jungles and up mountains, searching for locations to be used in survival TV programmes.

There have been some close calls. One night in the Namibian desert, Megan woke to find lions circling her campfire. Another time, while leading an expedition through Thailand, she stumbled upon a drug farm and was chased for hours by farmers armed with machine guns. She's been stalked by bears, bitten by snakes, and trapped by avalanches, but Megan wouldn't want any other kind of life.

What advice would she give to her younger self? Megan says, 'I would show her no matter how bizarre or far-fetched her dream is, there is a way to overcome the obstacles.'

SÓCRATES

(1954-2011)

Sócrates was born in Brazil, beside the mouth of the mighty Amazon river. He was named after the great Greek philosopher. When he was eight, Sócrates saw his father destroying the books in his library out of fear. Brazil was ruled by a military dictatorship and any material they didn't agree with could land you in prison. Sócrates never forgot this, and promised himself that he would fight oppression when he grew up.

When he got older, he went to play football for a team called Corinthians. A lot of football in Brazil was played by the rich but Sócrates's team had been started by a group of immigrant labourers in São Paulo.

He founded a group called Corinthians Democracy, which aimed to take on the brutal leaders of Brazil and win back some freedom for its people. The club won the championship in 1982, in shirts that had Democracia printed on them.

During his career, Sócrates was also studying for a degree in medicine. He qualified as a doctor in between training sessions and matches.

Dr Sócrates quickly gained a reputation as one of the best footballers in the world. He had a style that made it look as though he wasn't trying and he was always bouncing the ball off the back of his foot. Pelé once said that Sócrates played better going backwards than most players did going forwards.

He scored a lot of goals for Brazil internationally and became a hero. He spoke at a rally in front of 1.5 million people, saying that unless the government started free and fair elections, he'd move to Italy and play there. The government didn't listen. Sócrates went to Fiorentina.

Sócrates loved football but he never held it up as being anything other than a game. To him, people's freedom of expression was more important, and while football could help make that happen, it wasn't enough. He was named one of the best footballers ever to play, but he is remembered as much for his work off the pitch as what he did on it.

RONDA ROUSEY

(BORN 1987)

Ronda's birth was difficult and the complications meant she struggled to speak properly until she was six. Only a couple of years after she started talking, her father died.

She was raised by her mother, who was a judoka; a person who practises the martial art judo. Her mother wanted Ronda to learn to fight, too, so she started training her. By the time she was thirteen, Ronda was so strong she accidentally broke her mother's wrist.

But she struggled at school with how she looked; Ronda had skin problems, mangled ears from judo, and muscles from training. The other kids called her Miss Man. It hurt at the time, but a few years later, Ronda was the third most Googled person in the world. She knows now that being strong is nothing to be ashamed of.

'Fighting is not a man's thing,' she says. 'It's a human thing.'

Training with men bigger than her, Ronda became frustrated when she couldn't throw anyone. She says she cried almost every night of practice.

But it paid off.

When she was seventeen, Ronda became the youngest ever judoka in the Olympics. She went on to become the first American to win an Olympic medal at judo and the first woman to sign with the UFC: the Ultimate Fighting Championship. When she fought in the UFC, the average time it took her to win a match was two minutes and fifty-nine seconds. It seemed like no one could beat her.

Until one big fight, against Holly Holm, when Ronda unexpectedly lost and had to take time off to recover. But she didn't let it keep her down long.

Ronda's gone into professional wrestling now, fighting under the name Rowdy. Fans go wild whenever she steps into the ring.

No one calls her Miss Man now.

1729
$1+9\left(\frac{1}{4}\right)^4+17\left(\frac{1\times5}{4\times8}\right)^4+25\left(\frac{1\times5\times9}{4\times8\times12}\right)^4+\cdots$
$\frac{1}{\pi}=\frac{2\sqrt{2}}{9801}\sum_{k=0}^{\infty}\frac{(4k)!(1103+26390k)}{(k!)^4 396^{4k}}$

SRINIVASA RAMANUJAN

(1887-1920)

In 1913, an English mathematician called G. H. Hardy received a letter from India. 'Dear Sir,' it began. 'I beg to introduce myself to you as a clerk in the account department of the Port Trust Office of Madras on a salary of only twenty pounds per annum. I am now about twenty-three years of age.'

Along with the letter were pages and pages of mathematical theorems. At first, Hardy ignored them. But on closer inspection, he saw there was something special there. They were unlike anything he'd seen before. Hardy decided 'they must be true, because if they were not true, no one would have the imagination to invent them.'

Srinivasa had been devoted to maths ever since stumbling across an out-of-date textbook about elementary mathematics when he was sixteen. Before that, he'd been an excellent all-round student. Afterwards, he only cared about one thing: numbers. He failed every other subject.

Srinivasa ran away from home and relied on the hospitality of friends. He spent every waking hour scrawling ideas on scrap paper. Although it was clear to the locals how talented he was, the university wouldn't let him in. Instead he took a low-paying job in a bank.

With a recommendation letter from Hardy, Srinivasa was able to finally get a place at Madras University. Sometime later, Hardy also convinced Srinivasa to come and study at Cambridge University. After three seasick days on a steamer, he arrived in England.

Srinivasa was soon impressing everyone. The discoveries he made were mind-boggling and he was rewarded with degrees as well as becoming the first Indian to be inducted into the Royal Society.

But the cold weather and strange food of England were bad for his health. Srinivasa moved back to India, where he died at just thirty-two.

A lot of Srinivasa's ideas were so complex they have only been proved after his death. He has left behind piles of work that are still being pondered over by mathematicians today.

ROSIE SWALE-POPE

(BORN 1946)

On her fifty-seventh birthday, Rosie left her cottage in Wales and set out on a 20,000-mile run around the world.

Rosie wasn't always so confident. When she was fourteen, she was sent to boarding school with lice in her hair, woolly tights, and huge knickers. She once got zero out of a hundred in a test. Being outdoors always interested her more.

As she grew up, Rosie spent her time sailing across oceans, running marathons through deserts and Arctic tundra, and riding horses through entire countries.

When her husband died of prostate cancer, she set out on her round-the-world marathon expedition with the aim of letting people know they should get tested for the disease before it's too late. Beginning in the small seaside town of Tenby, she made her way across Europe, Russia, Alaska, Canada, and finally Iceland, before returning home five years later.

Along the way, she was chased by wolves, roared at by bears, threatened with guns and axes, hit by a bus, ill with pneumonia, and stuck in a blizzard. She pulled everything she needed along behind her in a trailer and spent nights either camping under the stars or staying with people she'd met. By the time Rosie got home, she was walking on crutches because she'd fractured her hip. Hundreds of people turned out to welcome her back to Tenby.

Rosie wants to encourage people to do things they wouldn't ordinarily do. It could be anything: jump out of a plane, ride a horse, or just make someone else's day special when yours isn't going too well.

'It began as a journey of loneliness and heartbreak,' Rosie said, 'but along the way it became about humanity. My message is, life is precious.'

STANISLAV PETROV

(1939-2017)

There is one man we may all have to thank for our lives. Most people will never know his name.

In 1983, Stanislav was manning a Russian command centre meant to monitor whether or not America was launching nuclear missiles. It was the height of the Cold War and the two powers had been locked in bitter arguments for decades. If America attacked, Russia would be ready to respond with the full force of its nuclear arsenal.

Stanislav Petrov was an engineer who was brought in one evening to work on the computer in the command centre, because the usual officer had been unable to turn up for duty. Late that night, the computer started flashing. It showed a missile had been launched from America. And another. And another.

The protocol was to alert the top commanders so they could begin immediate retaliation.

But instead, Stanislav paused. Unlike the others who worked at the command centre, he was not a soldier who had been trained to blindly obey orders. He could tell the computer wasn't perfect. The alerts it was giving out seemed too clear and certain to be true.

Stanislav called the command centre and told them the computer was broken. If he was wrong, his country was about to be decimated by nuclear weapons. He waited nervously for twenty-three minutes. It became clear that there had never been any missiles heading for Russia.

By not doing what he was supposed to do, Stanislav had prevented disaster.

It wasn't until ten years after the incident that the world found out what Stanislav had done. Thanks to his one decision, he probably avoided a Third World War, saved millions of lives, and changed the fate of planet earth. Who knows where we'd be today if Stanislav had acted differently? When he died, newspapers called him 'the man who saved the world'.

SALLY RIDE

(1951-2012)

As a teenager, Sally spent most of her time playing tennis and was soon one of the best in the country. She could have made it to the World Championships but realized that what she really wanted to do was pursue astrophysics: the study of stars, planets, and galaxies.

After graduating, Sally saw an advert in a newspaper that said for the first time in history, NASA was recruiting female astronauts. Seeing that advert, Sally knew her life was about to change forever. This was the opportunity she'd been waiting for.

Over eight thousand people applied and six women, including Sally, were chosen. They underwent exhausting training. For twelve-hour days, over two years, the recruits had to parachute jump, scuba-dive, fly jets, learn every corner of a spaceship, and study the intricate details of geology. Sally excelled and was chosen for a place on the space shuttle *Challenger*.

When it was announced at a press conference that Sally would be going to space, the journalists asked her ridiculous questions: Do you cry when things go wrong? How will you go to the toilet? Do you wish you were a boy? Sally either laughed at them or ignored them entirely. She knew what she was capable of, and that it had nothing to do with her being a woman or a man.

On June 18th 1983, Sally became the first American woman in space.

Looking out at planet earth from inside a spaceship, Sally experienced a special feeling that only astronauts ever really get to feel. She could see that everyone she's ever known, every lion and grasshopper, every palace and supermarket, was standing on a single rock floating in space. It gave her a new perspective. She realized that we have to take care of our planet, because it's all we have.

'It was the most fun I'll ever have in my life,' Sally said.

In 2001, she created her own company that aimed to encourage girls to move into science. Six years after her death, it's still going strong.

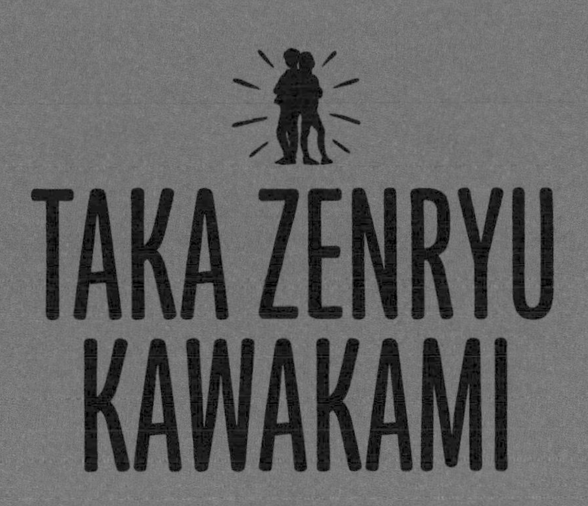

TAKA ZENRYU KAWAKAMI

Taka was born into a family that had created generations upon generations of priests for the Shunkoin temple in Kyoto, Japan. When he was young, it went without saying that he would become one too. But first he wanted to see America.

At university in Arizona, Taka studied religion and psychology. One day, while he was having tea with a friend, someone walked past and Taka made a rude comment about them being gay. His friend was shocked. 'I'm gay too,' they said. 'Is that the way you feel about me?'

Taka was ashamed. He thought of the discrimination he'd faced for being Asian in America. How could he face discrimination himself and then turn around and discriminate against others? Being gay was something Taka had never really thought about. When he did, he came to the conclusion that it was outlawed in Japan because they have a culture of everyone trying to be the same, to pass unnoticed, and not to be different.

Back in Japan, at the Shunkoin temple, Taka didn't forget his new values. Even though gay marriage is still illegal in Japan, he volunteered to perform marriages for same-sex couples at his temple. He's now married gay couples from around the world, as well as some from Japan.

Taka also gives talks at Japanese universities. He explains to students that same-sex relationships are nothing new in Japan, and there are records of them happening over two thousand years ago. There is also nothing in the sacred texts of Buddhism that prohibits such relationships.

'About seven per cent of people in Japan don't have the option to get married,' Taka said. 'This cannot lead to happiness in the country.'

With his help, we're already seeing a little more happiness spread through Japan.

SAVANNA KARMUE

(BORN 2006)

Savanna could barely believe it when she heard that heart disease kills over two thousand Americans every day. The saddest thing is that it doesn't have to be that way: if we look after our hearts, our hearts will look after us.

She'd gone to visit her Sunday school teacher in hospital after an operation and started talking to the cardiologists on the ward. She was only six but her curiosity led her to study, learning about veins and arteries, how oxygen and nutrients are pumped around the body through the blood, and how important it is to eat well and exercise regularly.

The more Savanna learned about the human heart, the more certain she became that one day she wanted to become a cardiologist. But she didn't want to wait. America is in the midst of an obesity epidemic, with around one in three kids being overweight, largely down to a diet of junk food and sugary drinks. Savanna wanted to help them as soon as possible.

She founded a charity called Happy Heart Advice, which aims to educate people about how best to keep their hearts healthy. The initial stage of her plan involved writing a book, which set out everything she'd learned in her research, so that other kids would have the benefit of what she'd found out.

The next stage of her charity involved setting up Happy Heart Challenges. Over periods of five to ten days, Savanna visits schools to teach students how to make healthy snacks, engage in exercise, and understand the cardiovascular system. She thinks they're more likely to listen to someone of their own age.

By 2031, Savanna hopes to have helped halve childhood obesity and the number of deaths from heart disease. She thinks we all deserve to have happy hearts.

THE INNOCENCE PROJECT

In 1986, a twenty-seven-year-old woman was found dead in New York City. Barry Gibbs was arrested. He was a postman who had fought in the Vietnam War and lived in New York all his life. When the police picked him up, Barry had no idea what was happening.

Barry was sentenced to twenty years in prison. He protested his innocence but no one believed him. Even his own son believed he'd committed the crime.

After years spent in jail, Barry was depressed, lonely, and desperate. He got in contact with the Innocence Project, pleading for help. When they searched for the DNA evidence related to his case, they found it had mysteriously disappeared.

Then, one day, the home of one of the men who had arrested Barry was searched and the evidence was found. Barry had been framed and they had proof. With the help of lawyers from the Innocence Project, Barry was set free after nineteen years in jail.

In 2010, the city of New York awarded Barry ten million dollars in compensation. Obviously it could never be enough to make up for what had happened to him, but it meant he could try and enjoy the years of freedom he had left.

The Innocence Project have helped hundreds of people like Barry without asking anything in return. They work tirelessly to find new DNA evidence that can set innocent prisoners free. Some of the prisoners they try and help have life sentences, others have been sentenced to death.

People can be convicted of things they haven't done for three main reasons: witnesses thought they saw things they didn't see, evidence wasn't treated carefully, and people were tricked into confessing to things they didn't do. Whatever the reason, Barry Schek, Peter Neufeld and their team of dedicated lawyers continue to fight for those they believe to be innocent.

SOPHIE BLANCHARD

(1778-1819)

In 1804, a Frenchwoman called Sophie Blanchard became the first female aeronaut in the world.

On the ground, Sophie was nervous and shy, too afraid to ride in horse-drawn carriages. In the air, though, she became intrepid. She filled her balloon with fireworks and let them off to the amazement of enthralled crowds. She sent dogs parachuting out of her basket. She even embarked on a treacherous balloon journey over the Alps, where frost froze her face and hands.

Sophie would often pass out from going far too high in her balloon. Sometimes, she would fly out at night and sleep in her balloon among the clouds.

The sky was where she felt most at home.

But it was also dangerous. Having fireworks so close to the flammable hydrogen gas meant the entire balloon could go up in flames at any time. Balloons were also notoriously difficult to control and Sophie often crash-landed. But the fearless woman and her balloon became famous all over France.

Napoleon made Sophie Chief Air Minister of Ballooning. He had plans to use balloons to attack his enemies in future wars, and wanted her help.

One day in July 1819, crowds gathered at the Tivoli Gardens in Paris. As Sophie's balloon rose, she lit fireworks and dropped them, so that they lit up beneath her like shooting stars.

All of a sudden, the sky flashed and flames engulfed the balloon. It rapidly began to sink. Cutting loose the ballast, Sophie thought she was going to make it, until she got caught on the side of a house and was thrown into the street below.

With that, Sophie also became the first woman to die in an aviation accident. She was buried in Paris, under a tombstone carved with the image of her balloon in flames.

XV

THE WHITE HELMETS

Every day, bombs fall on Syrian homes, hospitals and schools. Some contain old nails or pieces of metal and some contain poisonous gas. Most of the bombs are dropped by the Syrian government. They say they're targeting terrorists but it's ordinary people who are dying.

And when those ordinary people are trapped under the rubble of collapsed buildings, desperately calling for help, it's the White Helmets who risk their lives to save them.

The White Helmets, officially called Syria Civil Defence, come from many different backgrounds and religions; they range from engineers to painters and teachers to tailors. They are volunteers, without weapons, who help anyone who needs it, regardless of what side of the conflict they're fighting on.

The volunteers rescue trapped people, administer first aid, and recover bodies so they can be given proper burials. So far, they've saved over 114,431 lives.

In some very religious parts of Syria, it is forbidden for men to rescue women, and so two women's bands of the White Helmets have formed. After raising over $100,000 in donations, the women's arm of the operation now has six ambulances and one hundred volunteers.

The White Helmets also play a crucial role in capturing on video everything that has happened in Syria. Using their footage, organizations can work out whether bombs have been dropped on civilians. In April 2018, it was their recordings that proved the Syrian government had let off poison gas, killing eighty-three of their own people.

Due to political reasons, both the Russian and Syrian government have tried to spread lies about the White Helmets being linked to terrorists. It hasn't stopped them doing what they set out to do. They know a life saved is worth everything. Nothing will prevent them from trooping out during bomb raids to haul debris aside, searching for survivors.

SOPHIE PASCOE

(BORN 1993)

Sophie Pascoe was just two years old when her legs got caught in the blades of a lawnmower being driven by her father. It was a horrific accident that left her fighting for her life. Doctors managed to save her right leg, though her left one had to be amputated below the knee.

The accident left her a little timid at first. 'I can't do that,' she'd say, watching her older sister climb a tree or leap off a climbing frame.

'You can,' her parents would say. 'Just try.'

When swimming lessons started at school, Sophie struggled to keep up with the other kids, so her mum arranged for her to have one-on-one lessons.

Later that year, the school geared up for its annual swimming races. For the first time, Sophie raced against her classmates. She beat them all. It was proof to her that she could do more than just keep up with able-bodied people, she could shoot straight past them.

Everyone could see her talent. Before he passed away, her grandfather made Sophie promise that one day she would compete in the Paralympics and win a gold.

That's exactly what she set out to do.

By adhering rigidly to a gruelling training regime, Sophie unexpectedly qualified for the 2008 Beijing Paralympics. She was only fifteen years old. Her home country, New Zealand, was proud, but Sophie was so young that they didn't expect her to be able to compete with the other athletes. Just like in her first school race, Sophie soared above everyone's expectations. She won three gold medals and a silver.

Looking into each other's eyes as the medals were hung around her neck, Sophie and her father reached an unspoken understanding: there may have been an accident and it may have been harrowing, but look at her now – a world champion.

Sophie's still competing, training mercilessly and breaking records. She once promised her grandfather she'd win a gold medal. So far she's won nine.

THOMAS NEUWIRTH

(BORN 1988)

The Austrian village of Bad Mitterndorf sits among snow-capped mountains and rolling green meadows. For Thomas, it was a beautiful but lonely place to grow up in, especially after he realized he was more attracted to boys than girls. There was no gay community and no one to talk to about his feelings. He felt different and thought there was something wrong with him.

In the attic of his house, Thomas would dress up in skirts and dresses. It was only when he was alone that he felt he could be who he really was. Then, after moving to a bigger city and studying fashion, he began to feel more and more comfortable expressing himself. To show it, he created a character for himself named Conchita Wurst.

Conchita has dark, mysterious eyes, long, silky hair, and a perfectly-shaped beard. She dresses in glamorous dresses and sings in a roaring, tender voice.

On September 10th 2013, Conchita was chosen by Austria to represent them at the Eurovision song contest.

Many people rallied around Conchita, not just because of her beautiful performances, but because a vote for her would be a vote against homophobia and old-fashioned attitudes about how people should be.

There were some harsh comments, especially from countries where gay people still fight to earn the same rights as everyone else. But they didn't shake Conchita.

On the night of the Eurovision final, she appeared on stage in an intricate golden gown, and sang a song about battling through dark times, staying true to herself, and rising from the ashes like a phoenix.

With 290 points, Conchita became Austria's first Eurovision winner in over fifty years. As an audience of 170 million people around the world watched, she proudly raised the trophy and announced, 'We are unity and we are unstoppable.'

It was a victory, not just for Austria, not just for Conchita or Thomas, but for everyone who's ever felt like they didn't quite fit in.

THE TEACHER FROM THE ST NICOLAI KINDERGARTEN

It's a peaceful summer morning in Germany. The children of St Nicolai kindergarten head out on an adventure in the woods. It's a warm day and the vivid green trees are swaying gently in a cool breeze. Suddenly, a scream rings out. Someone has disappeared.

While playing with a pile of logs, a three-year-old boy has fallen through a panel of rotten wood covering an old coal mineshaft. The drop is twenty-five metres into a pool of deep water. The boy can't swim.

Without even thinking, his teacher throws herself into the darkness after him. She finds the boy and holds him to her chest. Scrabbling desperately, she finds something to hold onto on the wall of the mineshaft. The water is cold and dark and full of old pieces of rusty metal. Her body heat keeps the boy alive.

'We're okay,' she shouts up to the other children.

They wait together for an hour and a half. Finally, firefighters arrive to lift them both out of the pit. Neither of them are badly hurt.

'It may have been cold,' the firefighters say, 'but without the water, both of them would have crashed into the ground and died.'

Newspapers across Germany read: Brave Schoolteacher Saves Child From Drowning. That year, she is made Teacher of the Year and everyone in Germany is talking about the miracle in the Osterwald forest. Not wanting to draw attention to herself, the brave schoolteacher doesn't want anyone to know her name. The majority of the country might not know who she is, but they admire her for her courage and kindness regardless.

TSALI

In May 1838, Tsali's brother came to his cabin with urgent news. The white men from across the ocean were rounding up native Cherokee people and driving them off their land. Before the next new moon, all Cherokee must begin the long march west. If they refused, they could be killed.

Up until then, Tsali had lived a quiet life in a cabin by the Nantahala River, with his wife and three sons. He didn't see why he ought to move.

As soldiers scoured the land, thousands were forced out of their homes. Some managed to evade capture but Tsali wasn't so lucky. When the soldiers came across his house, they led him and his family away.

While they were travelling, Tsali's wife stumbled and one of the soldiers jabbed her with his bayonet. This made Tsali furious. In their own language, he told his people: When we reach the next turn, I shall pretend to have hurt my ankle. As the soldiers stop, leap on them and seize their guns. Then we shall escape to the mountains.

The plan worked, though one soldier was accidentally killed in the tussle. Tsali and his family fled and found refuge in a cave on the side of a mountain. There, they lived among other Cherokee who had been driven into hiding, making a vow never to abandon their homeland.

The army generals were humiliated. One of their own men had been killed. Their general proposed that if Tsali turned himself in, they would move on without hunting down the three hundred other Cherokee hiding in the Smoky Mountains.

Tsali gave himself up in exchange for the freedom of his people.

'It is sweet to die in one's native land,' Tsali said, while waiting to be shot, 'and to be buried by the margins of one's native stream.'

Over a hundred years later, the land was flooded, and Tsali's grave now lies beneath Fontana Lake. The three hundred Cherokee he saved became the ancestors of over five thousand Native Americans alive today.

TU YOUYOU

(BORN 1930)

In the 1960s, North Vietnam was in the midst of a chaotic war with the South. It wasn't only bullets and bombs the troops had to worry about. For soldiers picking their way through the deep rainforest, malaria was a far more pressing concern. Being bitten by a mosquito and contracting the disease would mean a high fever, vomiting, yellow skin, and quite possibly death.

Medicine existed but it was no longer working and scientists everywhere were trying and failing to find a cure. Desperate, the leader of North Vietnam went to the president of China and asked for his help. In response, a secret initiative called Project 523 was established. That was where Tu came in.

Tu had been inspired to go into medicine ever since contracting tuberculosis as a child. The experience made her want to understand disease so that she could keep herself healthy and help others too. At university, she studied not just modern medicine, but traditional Chinese herbal medicine too, believing that there was a lot to be learned from 2,500 years of history.

It was this experience of traditional medicine that Tu brought to Project 523. Scientists across the world had tested over 240,000 different compounds and none had worked. Under Tu's guidance, two hundred traditional Chinese recipes were concocted instead and tested on mice.

A small, spiky plant called sweet wormwood appeared to be effective on animals. Not wanting to endanger anyone else's life, Tu tested the treatment on herself first. It worked, completely eradicating her symptoms of tuberculosis.

Thanks to Tu's research, millions of lives were saved all across the developing world. In 2015, she was awarded the Nobel Prize. Many people saw it as a victory for traditional Chinese medicine, and proof that we still have a lot to learn from our ancestors.

VIDAL SASSOON

(1928-2012)

After his father left, Vidal, his brother, and his mother moved into a two-bedroom apartment with his aunt and her three children. They shared a freezing outside toilet with three other families.

His mother ended up sending Vidal and his brother to an orphanage, where they were bullied for being Jewish and struggled at school. When war broke out, the brothers were evacuated to the countryside.

Once he'd returned to London, Vidal dreamed of becoming a footballer. But his mother had other ideas. She dragged Vidal along to a hairdresser and asked if they had any jobs. The owner explained that Vidal would need to train for two years if he wanted to cut hair, and that the training would be expensive. Dejected, Vidal and his mother turned to leave.

'Wait,' the salon owner called out. 'You seem like a polite boy. You can start on Monday.'

It was then that Vidal decided if he was going to be a hairdresser, he was going to be a revolutionary one. He worked as hard as he could and dedicated himself to becoming the best.

By the time he was twenty-six, Vidal had his own salon. It was so small that people had to sit waiting on the stairs. They didn't mind. Talk of Vidal's talent had spread throughout the capital and everyone wanted an appointment.

Instead of relying on constant upkeep and expensive products, Vidal's haircuts were designed to fall naturally into place. They transformed lives. Women no longer spent hours every week sitting rigidly in salons under uncomfortable machines: instead they could get stunning haircuts that would last months.

Soon he was cutting the hair of actors and models, opening salons across the globe, and releasing his own line of haircare products. Vidal used his money to try and help Jewish people across the world.

URSULA K. LE GUIN

(1929-2018)

Ursula's parents were anthropologists, which meant they studied people from all around the world, and looked at what makes us human and what bonds us together. Her mother chronicled the last of the Yani people, a tribe of Native Americans who had once roamed the Sierra Nevada mountains. She was interested in how they had lived before colonists arrived from across the ocean and slaughtered them in order to take control of their lands.

The house was always full of books and Ursula began reading and writing at a young age. She sent off her first story when she was eleven, to a magazine called *Astounding Science Fiction*. It was rejected. As were all her stories for years to come. But she never gave up. It took ten years for a publisher to finally take notice.

When Ursula married and had children, her husband took over a lot of the housework and family duties so she had more time to write. She used the time to create Earthsea: a vast world made up of hundreds of islands, surrounded by uncharted expanses of ocean. In her stories, wizards wrestle weather, ancient dragons flatten settlements, and everything hangs in a delicate balance between land and sea, light and dark, and good and evil.

Once it was published, generations of children spent hours escaping to Earthsea, following the adventures of Sparrowhawk, a young wizard who left the peaceful island of Gont to study magic across the ocean.

In another book, Ursula created a race of people called Gethenians, who existed without gender. She wanted to explore how characters acted when they weren't expected to be boys or girls.

Using a different set of tools, Ursula explored the same deep questions her parents had. How should we be in the world? Are there other ways to live? What is fair?

When Ursula died in early 2018, people all over the planet stood up to thank her for the magic and wisdom she'd given to their lives.

WERNER HERZOG

(BORN 1942)

As a child, Werner refused to sing or play instruments at school and was almost expelled for it. All kinds of things would make him angry and he lost his temper easily. Most of the time, he preferred to be alone.

His family were so poor he barely knew cinema existed until a travelling projectionist visited his small village in Germany. Werner was hooked. He began writing scripts and hatching grand plans for epic films.

He still got angry because he looked young for his age. Even as he got older, he felt that film executives didn't take him seriously. He was frustrated because they saw him as a child.

He earned a scholarship to study literature and theatre in America. On the journey there, Werner met Martje, who would go on to become his wife.

After three days, Werner left the university. The US government said they were going to send him back to Germany if he wasn't studying, so he fled to Mexico.

In 1965, Werner returned to Germany. He stole a camera and made his first short film about four boys defending their crumbling fortress against an invisible enemy. It was the first of many strange and magical stories to come.

For one film, Werner had the actors recreate a doomed journey along the Amazon river made by Spanish conquistadors. The cast and crew had to live in huts on the riverbank, float along the river in badly built rafts, and survive the heat while wearing heavy historic clothing.

When 400 monkeys needed for the film were stolen, Werner pretended to be a vet to get them back. He refused to give up on anything or compromise any aspect his vision. Often, his temper would flare up when things weren't going right, and he had to learn to control himself in order to create his art.

Werner believes that storytelling is important. 'I try to be after something that is deeply reverberating inside of our souls,' he says.

By learning to control his temper, Werner has freed himself to go and create some of the strangest and most beautiful films ever made.

VERA RUBIN

(1928-2016)

Everything we can see in our universe, from planets to ladybirds, is made of matter built from atoms. But scientists believe that eighty-five per cent of all matter is a different, mysterious substance called dark matter. We know almost nothing about dark matter, only that it must exist. The first person to realize its existence was a woman named Vera Rubin.

As a child, Vera would lie awake at night, gazing out through her window at the stars. Wanting to get a closer look, she built her own telescope with the help of her father.

In 1948, Vera was the only astronomy major to graduate from her college. She was told that some universities didn't accept women in her field. Eventually she found a place, earned a degree, and began teaching and researching.

Together with a scientist called Kent Ford, Vera examined the light coming to us from stars in distant galaxies. The more they learned, the more things didn't quite make sense. The stars were moving too quickly for the amount of matter contained in them. Vera reasoned that the only way to explain it would be if most of the matter in these distant galaxies was invisible; if most of the matter was dark matter.

Scientists were hesitant to agree at first as the theory was so outlandish. But the evidence was unarguable. It's now almost universally accepted, even if we still have no idea quite what dark matter is.

Vera continued to explore the universe. In 1992 she discovered a galaxy in which half the stars orbited in one direction, and the others went in the opposite direction. She believed this galaxy may be the result of two separate galaxies colliding and merging together!

'Still more mysteries of the universe remain hidden,' Vera once said. 'Their discovery awaits the adventurous scientists of the future.'

WILLIAM BUCKLAND

(1784-1856)

William lived in a small market town in Devon surrounded by old quarries and bright fields. His father was a vicar and would often take his son on walks through the countryside, where William scoured the ground for glimpses of the distant past in fossils, ammonites, and Jurassic rock.

At university, William studied Christianity like his father, but he explored geology and mineralogy too. He believed that the earth beneath our feet held secrets and he was determined to find out what those secrets were.

After becoming a priest, William continued his investigations into what makes up the earth.

While excavating Kirkdale Cave in 1821, William unearthed the bones of countless creatures now extinct in Britain, like the hyena, elephant, hippo, and rhino. At first he thought the skeletons had been washed up there during the great flood of the Bible. Then, on closer inspection, he could see that the hyenas had been dragging the other animals there to eat them.

William was certainly different. Even while out digging for remains and examining rock faces, he preferred to wear an academic gown. He owned a table made out of fossilized dinosaur poo. Students have said that he would sometimes choose to give his lectures while sitting on the back of a horse.

When he got married, William's honeymoon lasted an entire year, and was spent in the pits and caves of Europe with his wife, Mary.

One day, at the Geological Society of London, William announced the discovery of an unheard-of species of giant reptile that walked the earth 166 million years ago. He called the reptile Megalosaurus. It was the first example of the creatures scientists would later call dinosaurs.

When William died, the site set aside for his burial was found to contain Jurassic limestone. It needed to be blown up before William could be laid to rest. Friends saw it as the final joke of a dedicated scientist who never took himself too seriously.

WHOOPI GOLDBERG

(BORN 1955)

Whoopi couldn't believe it the first time she saw a black woman on the TV. The woman was Nichelle Nichols and she was playing Uhura, a communications officer living onboard the USS *Enterprise* as it battled its way through deep space.

Whoopi knew she wanted to be an actor. Seeing Uhura in *Star Trek*, she knew it was possible too.

With her dad gone and her mum always at work, Whoopi was on her own a lot. She became obsessed with movies, and would spend entire days watching them back to back.

As soon as she could, she moved to California to begin her acting career. She wasn't moving alone – she had her newborn daughter to care for, too. To support her, Whoopi worked in a bank, laid bricks, and even put make-up onto dead bodies at a funeral home. For years, she worked during the day and spent her nights and weekends performing in theatres. She never stopped acting because acting allowed her to escape life and pretend to be someone else for a while.

Whoopi created a one-woman show called *The Spook Show*, in which she portrayed various strange characters of her own creation. The characters were all misfits and oddballs, people who didn't quite fit in, and whose ways of seeing the world proved hilarious and heartbreaking. Everyone loved it.

Through *The Spook Show*, Whoopi got a part in *The Color Purple*, a film that chronicled the struggle of an African-American woman living in America in the 1930s. Since then, she's played a psychic who can commune with ghosts, a nun with a beautiful singing voice, and an evil ice queen.

Eventually, Whoopi got her own role in *Star Trek*, playing a wise alien from the planet Nova Kron. Now she cruises through deep space on the USS *Enterprise*, inspiring young girls to pursue their dreams.

WITOLD PILECKI

(1901-1948)

Witold Pilecki fought during the First World War, defending Poland against the Russians. When the Second World War began and the Nazis invaded Poland, conquering the Polish army, Witold's days of military service began again.

Together with another soldier, Witold formed the Secret Polish Army, which was soon made part of the larger Polish resistance. The men and women of the resistance maintained cover, working normal jobs so as not to arouse the suspicions of occupying Nazis.

One day Witold came to his superiors with a plan. There had been much talk of a giant camp called Auschwitz that had been built in the south of Poland and no one was quite sure what went on there. Witold volunteered to be arrested and sent to the camp so that he could find out more information.

Once there, Witold soon discovered to his horror that Auschwitz wasn't a prison, but a death camp, purposely built to kill Jewish people on a large scale using poisonous gas.

Using parts smuggled into the camp, Witold built a radio transmitter which he could use to send information to the resistance. He also wrote long reports by hand which would then be snuck out of the camp and sent to the British government. Thanks to his bravery, Witold became the first person to alert the outside world of the Nazis' atrocities.

After three years of undercover observation, it was time to leave. During the night shift at a bakery, Witold and two other prisoners cut the alarm and telephone wires, took down their guard and escaped. They scattered tobacco behind them as they fled, so that the Nazis' dogs wouldn't be able to follow their scent.

Witold was eventually arrested by communist authorities. They charged him with spying and sending information to the British. For this, Witold was executed.

It wasn't until 1990 that Witold's huge contribution to our understanding of just how cruel the Nazis had been was revealed. Since then, a monument has been built so that nobody would forget him, and schools and streets across Poland have been named after Witold: the man who volunteered for Auschwitz.

ZULMA BRANDONI DE GASPARINI

(BORN 1944)

Gasparinisaura was a small, plant-eating dinosaur that walked on two legs and balanced itself with a long tail. Eighty-three million years ago, it roamed what is now South America in small herds. Gasparinisaura is one of the few dinosaurs to be named with the feminine 'saura' rather than the masculine 'saurus'. Why? Because it was named after a woman called Zulma Brandoni de Gasparini.

Growing up in Argentina in the 1950s, it was unthinkable that Zulma would become a scientist. Women were expected to stay at home, doing housework and looking after children. But Zulma didn't let that get in the way of her studying zoology at the university of La Plata.

When she went to continue her studies at the Miguel Lillo Institute, she was warned away from studying the fossils of marine reptiles. The other scientists claimed it was too complex for her to understand. Zulma ignored them.

She wrote to a university in America, seeking information on fossil records, and began her own exhaustive research. Travelling between Argentina, Cuba, Colombia, Venezuela, and Antarctica, she hunted tirelessly for fossils. By examining the skeletons of marine creatures that lived millions of years ago, Zulma helped to piece together a picture of what our world once looked like.

When Zulma discovered the Gasparinisaura, it was quickly decided that the creature ought to be named after the woman who had done so much to further our understanding of life on earth. Today, Zulma teaches at the National University of La Plata, encouraging a new generation of young women to pursue the mysteries of the dinosaurs.

YUAN LONGPING

(BORN 1930)

In the 1960s, tens of millions of people died in China due to a famine. A combination of bad weather, natural disasters and poor economy meant that there just wasn't enough food to go around. People ate everything they could: grass, clay, roots, and even sometimes each other.

Yuan was horrified. He had been born to a poor family and had graduated from a farming college. One night, Yuan dreamed of towering rice plants, taller than any that had been seen in China before. It gave him an idea. As rice is the main staple of the Chinese diet, he thought that the key to preventing future famine would be to work out a way of producing more of it.

Yuan's idea was to breed two different kinds of rice together into a new kind of hybrid rice that might provide more food. The first experiments did create a new kind of rice but it had no benefits over the old. Next Yuan tried breeding the rice with wild rice rather than the common cultivated variety. The results were unbelievable.

The new rice would yield twenty per cent more than the previous rice breeds. China's rice output quadrupled between 1950 and 2017, to almost 200 million tons. The increase each year was enough to feed an extra sixty million people.

Yuan hasn't stopped working. Now he's trying to create an even more productive kind of rice that will feed countless people across the globe.

Every day, Yuan rides out on his motorbike through his rice fields. He will never know how many millions of lives he may have saved; all he knows is that he wants to save more.

was born in 1992 and lives in Berlin.
He is the author of several books,
including *Grow Up* and *Lolito*, which won
the Somerset Maugham Award in 2015.
He is the author of the international bestseller
Stories for Boys Who Dare To Be Different.

QUINTON WINTER

is a British illustrator, artist and colourist.
He has worked for many clients including
the *Guardian* newspaper, Walker Books,
'Gogglebox', *2000AD*, Vertigo Comics,
Mojo and the BBC. He is the illustrator
of the international bestseller
Stories for Boys Who Dare To Be Different.